The Prison Cure

Reform Beyond Incarceration

Written By: Jesse J. Jacoby

Soulspire Publishing
Truckee, CA, 96161

ISBN: 978-1-968660-31-4
Library of Congress Control Number: 2012921011
Dewey CIP: 641.563   **OCLC:** 213839254

Cover art, font, and layout by: Soulspire Publishing

Wholesalers to book trade: Nelson's Books and Ingram
Available through Amazon.com, BarnesAndNoble.com

Dedication

This book represents the people who were thrown away before they were ever understood. All the brothers who sat in silence with dreams that no one asked them to speak. To the sisters who carried whole families on their backs, endured fluorescent nights and strip searches, and still braided hope into every day they survived. For the children who became inmates before they ever had a childhood. For the souls who were punished when they really needed to be purified.

These pages reflect the embers of faith that every man, woman, and youth who has been caged, mislabeled, and forgotten carries for a brighter reality. This work is for you.

To those who never had a teacher, a father, or a meal that fed the light in them. To those who held on to their will through noise, steel, hunger, and humiliation. To those who are still trying, still waking up, and still believing in a better way.

You are not your past. You are not your paperwork. You are not what they did to you. You are potential in motion. You are healing in progress. You are worthy of nourishment, of dignity, of redemption.

This is for the ones who have been told a thousand times who they are and are finally ready to remember who they have always been.

Acknowledgments

To those who have lived through the bars, both visible and unseen, this book was born from your strength, your scars, and your sacred potential.

To the brothers I walked beside on cold concrete, and to the sisters who wrote letters from locked-down dreams. Thank you for your stories, your courage, and your unwavering humanity.

To the healers, mentors, and revolutionaries who dare to see beyond the label of *"inmate"* and into the soul of the becoming man or woman, you are the midwives of a new way. Thank you for believing in redemption, not just retribution.

To the plants, the Earth, the sun, the breath, and the body's innate wisdom. Thank you for teaching me that true freedom begins within.

To my family and those who never stopped loving me, even when I had forgotten how to love myself. Your faith lit the way back.

To the people who are still sitting behind walls, wondering if anyone cares: *I see you. I wrote this for you.* May this work be a lantern in your tunnel and a seed in your soil.

Finally, to the Divine Orchestration that moves through all things, visible and invisible, thank you for not letting my story end in a cage.

This is not just a book. This is a vow. A vow to return with keys.

The Map to Reform

Introduction: A System Built to Break or a Pathway to Heal?

The machinery of the system is built for compliance, not transformation. This will polish the shell while letting the spirit starve. When I was just fourteen years old, I was incarcerated in the Department of Corrections. A child. A soul in formation. I had already fallen through so many cracks that by the time they put handcuffs on me, this felt less like punishment and more like confirmation: *this is where they send the forgotten.*

At sixteen, I was sent to a Gateway Youth Home. By then, I had learned how to follow rules better than I had ever been taught how to heal. I became house coordinator, the top role in the system, managing duties, navigating responsibilities, and even visiting the adult facility for supplies. Yet, with all that structure, no one ever asked me how I was doing inside. No one offered real food. No one offered purpose. I was conditioned for compliance, not transformation.

Later in life, when I was twenty-eight, I found myself back in prison. This time for cannabis, a plant that is now legal in much of the country. I was sent to a prison boot camp where torture passed for *"rehabilitation,"* and where dehumanization was relentless and refined. I survived, but not unchanged. I left with a vow: *No one should have to go through what I went through to wake up. No one should be caged and poisoned and called "reformed."*

That is why this book exists. The Prison Cure is more than a proposal. This is a lifeline. A declaration that real reform is not just possible, but necessary. A challenge to the very architecture of incarceration. An invitation to reimagine incarceration not as punishment, but as potential. We all know the current model is not working and cannot facilitate healing. This is not reforming, but is perpetuating a cycle of sickness, poverty, and punishment.

The daily meals inside prisons are not nourishing. They are slow poison. Mystery meat. White bread. Packets of sugar. GMO slop served on Styrofoam trays, stacked high and trashed by the thousands every single day, in every single prison. The waste alone is staggering. A single medium-sized prison can generate hundreds of pounds of garbage per day. Multiply that by over 5,000 correctional facilities in the U.S., and you begin to see the picture. Landfills are overflowing. Bodies are decaying. Nothing about this system is sustainable. Not environmentally, not nutritionally, and certainly not spiritually.

Then there is the commissary scam. The illusion of choice. Inmates are offered chips, ramen, soda, candy, processed beef sticks, and synthetic supplements. All are supplied by corporations that profit from addiction, not health. The vendors are not healers. They are dealers of dependency. When someone has that as their only source of nourishment for months or years on end, how can we expect them to rise out of the hole they have been thrown in?

The truth is, once you are inside the system, the system wants to keep you there. They do not just strip your freedom. They feed you the very things that weaken your mind, your immune system, and your will. They engineer your stagnation. Your conditions keep you numb, sick, inflamed, and angry. This is not reform. This is refinement of punishment. This is oppression dressed up in the clothes of justice and language of law.

What if prison, instead, became a sanctuary of restoration? What if organic food rich with living enzymes replaced processed sludge? What if every prisoner drank clean water instead of chemical tap? What if trades, languages, music, and creative expression were daily bread? What if the body learned yoga and martial arts instead of only tension and fear? What if trauma therapy was as common as lockdown counts, and breathwork was used to dissolve rage instead of cages?

When we forget that every person carries a seed of goodness, we begin to treat them only as the sum of their mistakes, but a seed does not reveal the fruit in a day. This sprouting of life requires soil, water, sunlight, and time. If we offer only concrete and poison, the seed cannot germinate and bloom. Yet even then, the enclosed shell does not disappear but waits for better conditions. The work of reform is not to punish the seed for being buried, but to create what is required for growth.

This is the vision of The Prison Cure, rooted in my own survival. My presentation is built on everything I have lived, everything I have learned, and everything I now teach through SoulSpire. A sanctuary for healing through nourishment, movement, and truth. I have seen what happens when someone is given the right environment. They do not just recover, they remember who they really are.

This book is a map out of the current system and into a future where the human spirit is honored, even behind bars. Where time served becomes time transformed. Where our tax dollars go to empowering people, not destroying them. True public safety comes not from punishment, but from fulfilled potential. If we wish to create a society worth living in, we must begin at the roots. Where pain begins, where hope hides, and where the light, however faint, still flickers.

Part I: The System That Sickens

Before we can heal the wound, we must understand the weapon.

They say prison exists to punish, to correct, and to reform, but what if these walls are less a correctional institution and more a mirror reflecting a culture already unwell? The sickness begins long before the bars slam shut. Prior to a sentence being read, there is an invisible chain of causes: *trauma buried in childhood, opportunities denied, nourishment withheld, and stories of worthiness never told.*

No one stumbles into a cell without first stumbling through neglect. That version of neglect is designed through manufactured culture. Not necessarily by a single hand, but by the machinery of a society that has learned how to perpetuate through repetition, not redemption.

This part of the book is not written to assign blame, but to bring sight. Without naming the forces that fracture us, being poverty, processed food, the numbing lure of pharmaceuticals, racial injustice, and generational wounds passed like heirlooms, we will remain a people forever treating symptoms while the disease deepens.

Here, we will expose the machinery. The quiet gears of oppression that hum beneath the noise of the nightly news. The way corporations' profit from a body in chains, a mind in pain, and a spirit subdued. How broken food leads to broken focus. How broken focus feeds broken choices. How broken choices feed a system that thrives on them.

This is where the myth of *"rehabilitation"* begins to dissolve. This is where we admit, truthfully, that no cell, no guard, and no court have the power to heal what has not been nourished. This is where we begin to reclaim the tools of our own restoration.

The path to freedom, real freedom, does not begin at the prison gate. This starts in the soil where the seed of suffering is first planted. If we are to tend that soil, we must first be willing to dig.

To see clearly is an act of healing. When we bring awareness to the roots of suffering, we begin to loosen their grip. Society teaches us to look only at the surface. The crime, the cell, or the statistic. Wisdom asks us to look underneath. Beneath every act of harm is a history of harm endured. Beneath every hardened face is a heart that once longed to be seen. When we can look with this kind of vision, punishment no longer feels like justice, and compassion no longer feels like weakness. We cannot heal what we refuse to see.

Gateway 1: The Disease of Incarceration

How the System Creates the Very Sickness They Claim to Cure

You feel a reduction in frequency the moment you step inside. The gray walls, artificial light, and plastic air. The buzzing fluorescence that never lets the nervous system rest. Something in your body knows: *this is not a place for healing or regeneration.* Nothing seems real.

Prisons are marketed as facilities of correction. Institutions designed to reform behavior, instill accountability, and return better citizens to society. This is not what they do. Not in practice. Not in design. Not in the day-to-day lived experience of the millions of human beings who move through them.

Prisons in America are more than overpopulated. They are overloaded with toxicity. Nutritional, emotional, environmental, and spiritual degradation. We are not rehabilitating people; we are warehousing trauma. We are caging potential. Most insidiously, we are normalizing a culture where pain is punishment and healing is nowhere in sight.

What We Feed the Body, We Feed the Mind

The average meal served in prison is a cocktail of inflammation served on Styrofoam trays, stacked thousands deep and discarded daily.

General meals include:

• Genetically modified corn-based fillers.

• Processed meat from factory farms.

• Powdered eggs and ultra-processed soy slop.

• Refined sugar, hydrogenated oil, iodized salt, canola oil, and artificial flavorings.

These meals are not just lacking nutrients; they actively worsen chronic conditions. High blood pressure, obesity, diabetes, depression, skin disease, liver stress, and gut dysbiosis are epidemics inside the prison population. The worst part is there is no way out. Even the commissary, the supposed *"choice"*, offers no real escape. This is poison behind a price tag. The items offered on this list range from cancer causing to diabetes inducing and are major contributors to inflammation and sickness.

We do not just punish people with confinement. We punish them with deficiency.

Trauma Compounded by Toxins

Long before a conviction is stamped on paper, most who enter prison have already been sentenced by life itself. Childhood abuse, poverty, addiction, violence, and abandonment are the seeds planted in unguarded soil. Prison does not remove these roots but waters them with poison. Elevated cortisol from constant threat. Meals stripped of life, and laden with chemicals. Sleep fractured by noise and surveillance. Days starved of sunlight and contact with the living earth. All this steeped in the unspoken knowledge that one's body, choices, and dignity belong to someone else.

This is a chemistry of despair that hardens the heart, dulls the light of serotonin, clouds the mind, and leaves the spirit brittle. Reflection is not nurtured here, only reaction. Repentance is not fostered, only compliance. In this terrain, survival mode becomes the native tongue, and the nervous system rewires itself around vigilance and defense. What emerges from years in such conditions is not a healed human, but a human trained to live as if every day is a battlefield. This is not rehabilitation. This is dehumanization engineered with precision.

In such an environment, even the smallest ember of self-belief struggles to stay lit. Without access to nourishing food, clean water, or the quiet where the mind can untangle, a person's inner compass begins to spin. Hope becomes a luxury, not a lifeline. The body, inflamed and underfed, sends signals of exhaustion to a mind already carrying decades of pain. Spiritually, this is a famine. An intentional scarcity of beauty, connection, and meaning. When the soil of the soul is starved for too long, weeds of bitterness and resignation take root. The tragedy is not just what prison takes from a person's present but what is stolen from their future capacity to love, trust, and belong.

The Waste of a Wasted System

Now we can learn more about the excess waste produced in jails, institutions, and prisons. Not just of human life, but literal garbage. Every day in the U.S., hundreds of thousands of Styrofoam trays are used once and tossed. Multiply that by three meals a day, across thousands of prisons, jails, and juvenile centers. We are talking millions of toxic, non-biodegradable trays per week, heading straight to landfills and incinerators. This material does not go away.

Prisons are not just producing social and spiritual decay; they are massive contributors to environmental degradation. Plastic utensils, individually wrapped food packs, excessive packaging, and institutional disposables create an avalanche of waste, all funded by public tax dollars. No one talks about this, but we should.

Reform does not just mean reforming the inmate, this also applies to reforming the institution. The inputs and outputs. The entire culture of consumption and control.

Why the System Keeps You Sick

In the current model, inmates are not meant to heal. Not truly. Healing would mean liberation, first of the body, then of the mind, and eventually of the entire person. Liberation does not serve the machinery. The prison industry profits from return customers. From recidivism. From bodies bent just enough to re-enter, but not enough to revolt.

The design is subtle, but fingerprints are everywhere. The food is made to pacify, not energize. Starches that bloat, sugars that spike and crash, and synthetic additives that keep the nervous system in a haze. The routine is made to fragment the day into meaningless blocks of time, where the spirit forgets the arc of the story. The environment is made to suppress the very qualities that would allow someone to rise, being curiosity, self-worth, trust in others, and trust in self.

This is not accidental. We are experiencing deliberate architecture of imprisonment. A structure designed to subdue, sedate, and keep the human being in a state of managed deterioration. When the body is weakened, the mind clouded, and the spirit discouraged, the will to change is easily contained.

Yet, I believe in the human capacity to transmute even this. I have lived through these corridors of corrosion. I have felt the weight of a schedule meant to strip the meaning from my days. I have also seen what happens when the smallest seeds of true healing are planted in the most desolate soil. A single breath taken with awareness can be the beginning of sovereignty. A single act of kindness in a place of hostility can ignite the memory of our shared humanity.

That is the essence of *The Prison Cure*. Not naïve optimism but lived proof. Any place, no matter how dark, can become a space of transformation when the right elements are introduced. I propose changes not only to nutrition but to the very scaffolding of prison life. Imagine meals drawn from the earth, organic produce rich with living enzymes, grains unstripped of minerals, and clean water free of chemicals. Imagine days punctuated not by the clang of gates but by moments of breathwork, meditation, movement, and connection. Practices that rewire the nervous system for peace instead of hypervigilance. Imagine each person having a role that matters, a skill to cultivate, a craft to refine.

In the chapters ahead, we will explore these elements in detail. We will reclaim them from the wasteland of neglect and replant them in the soil of possibility. We will see how food becomes medicine, how breath becomes anchor, how movement becomes liberation, and how purpose becomes the spine of a man's return to himself.

The path forward is a choice. We can choose to leave things as they are, to continue the slow grinding of bodies and spirits into the dust, or we can choose to reimagine correctional facilities as gardens for human potential.

Gateway 2: Processed People, Processed Food

How We Feed the Incarcerated Shapes Who They Become

There is quiet violence happening in every prison cafeteria, every commissary transaction, and every meal tray dropped through a slot in the door. A distinguished type that does not scream, beat or bruise. This abuse poisons slowly, under the radar, meal by meal. This is the violence of food that disconnects a person from vitality, from self-respect, and from the possibility of healing.

If you want to understand the root of the crisis in prison reform, start with what is on the plate.

The Menu of Modern Incarceration

Prison food is not food in any true sense of the word. It is synthetic fuel designed for compliance, not health. It is industrial byproduct dressed up as a meal. All of this arrives on Styrofoam trays, with plastic utensils that snap under pressure, and paper cups filled with tap water that smells like bleach and other chemicals.

This food lacks the one ingredient every human being needs most: *life force.*

On any given day, an inmate might be served:

• Slimy processed meat molded from scraps and fillers.

• Sugar-laden fruit cocktail from aluminum cans.

• Bleached white bread, GMO soy grits, fake cheese.

• Instant mashed potatoes with hydrogenated oils.

• Powdered eggs, imitation syrup, and corn syrup-based juice drinks.

What We Eat, We Become

When you feed someone food with no enzymes, no fiber, no minerals, no color, and no vitality, you are not just starving their body, you are starving also their will. You are training their biology in a state of chronic fatigue, inflammation, and mental fog. Inmates do not just get malnourished; they become chemically dependent on the very substances that exacerbate their emotional volatility:

• Sugar highs followed by crashes.

• Caffeine and sodium binges followed by depression and dehydration.

• Yeast and processed carbs that feed candida and destroy gut integrity.

This is no coincidence that so many inmates struggle with rage, addiction, anxiety, and depression. The gut-brain axis is broken before they even get a chance to speak in court.

The Commissary Trap

The prison commissary is advertised as choice. In truth, this is another layer of control where processed poison is sold as privilege. There are no green juices. There are no apples or oranges. There is no fresh food. You can't buy your way out of sickness behind bars. You can only manage your descent—slowly, painfully, and expensively.

What can you buy with your limited funds?

• Chips, candy, ramen, soda.

• Processed "protein" bars with more chemicals than nutrients.

• Powdered drink mixes with aspartame and red dye 40.

• Beef sticks and sugary pastries.

• Packaged "vitamin" pills that do nothing to nourish.

Corporate Contracts, Human Costs

Behind the scenes, private corporations profit from these poison contracts. They strike deals with states to supply the lowest-bid food, regardless of quality. They make millions from commissary markups, phone fees, and privatized medical care. Inmates become customers in a closed-loop system they cannot exit.

The message is clear: *your body is our revenue stream.* Your health? *Optional.* Your future? *Not our concern.* This is not just negligent. This is a moral crime.

What If We Fed People to Heal?

Nourishment is a human right, not a luxury. In a space like prison, where almost every other form of power is stripped away, food may be the only place where dignity can begin to return. Imagine a prison where the food served was designed not to subdue, but to strengthen. What would happen to the prison culture? You would see inflammation drop, tempers would cool, and inmates would be thinking clearly for the first time in years.

What if inmates were served:

• Fresh vegetables from an on-site greenhouse.

• Whole grains that were sprouted and cooked with intention.

• Clean water that has been mineralized and filtered.

• Healing herbs like turmeric, nettle, and ginger.

• Enzyme-rich fruits, seeds, and fermented foods.

• A rainbow of nutrients instead of a palette of beige.

Food Reform Is Justice Reform

We cannot talk about rehabilitation if we are feeding people the very things that strip them of their biological capacity to regenerate. You cannot meditate your way out of neuroinflammation or journal your way through a candida bloom or a collapsing microbiome. Food is the foundation, the first reform, and the first act of recognition that someone's life still matters.

If we want people to rise from the ashes of incarceration, we must stop burying them in processed sludge. We must give them the tools to repair, not just their behavior, but their bodies, minds, and spirits. This begins with what is on the tray. This includes the food options available in communities where people live before their convictions.

To offer real food is to say: *I see you as human.* A meal filled with life force is not only nutrition but is recognition. This tells the body; *you are worth healing, and* reminds the spirit, *you are worth remembering.* When food is alive, the one who is eating is also invited to come alive.

The wisdom of the body cannot be separated from the wisdom of the mind. When we feed the body with poison, the mind begins to decay. When we feed the body with light, the mind clears, and the heart remembers your rhythm. Food is more than matter. What we ingest carries vibration, memory, and intention. To change what we serve is to change the story of what a person can become.

If we begin with nourishment, we begin with dignity. When a person receives a meal that honors their life, they can slowly begin to honor life themselves. This is not a luxury. This is the soil from which every other form of transformation must grow. Food reform is not separate from justice reform. This is justice embodied in the most ordinary act. A tray set down with care, carrying the possibility of renewal.

When we serve food that heals, we are not just filling stomachs, but we are also planting futures. Each bite becomes a lesson in belonging, each tray a small covenant that says: *your life is still worthy of care.* This is why food reform matters so deeply: *because this is tangible, immediate, and daily.* Three times a day, we have the chance to reinforce despair or to awaken dignity. Reform is not some distant policy; but is the meal in front of a man whose hope has grown thin.

Food is the first doorway to transformation because this is the most intimate, and upon entering the body becomes blood, becomes thought, and becomes choice. If we saturate prisons with chemicals and processed sludge, then violence, depression, and numbness are predictable outcomes. If we nurture them with enzymes, minerals, and living nourishment, then healing, clarity, and peace become possible outcomes too. The future of justice is not built in courtrooms or cages, but in gardens, kitchens, and the sacred ritual of breaking bread with respect.

Gateway 3: What I Lived Through

From Caged Youth to Conscious Man

They never asked who I was when they locked me up at fourteen. I was placed on the *"incoming freshman list"* of kids who they target for the prison industry as I was entering high school. They do not question what you have been through, or what you have seen. There is no concern with what you have lost. They are conditioned to see a *"juvenile delinquent"* and hand over a sentence. What they are truly sentencing is a soul still trying to figure out how to find their way.

The First Cage

At fourteen, I was navigating trauma, confusion, and a world that did not feel safe, and instead of support or mentorship, I got shackles. I was a kid, barely beginning to understand myself, when I was thrown into the Department of Corrections. The name sounds official, and clinical, but nothing about that experience corrected me. I did see that power can be abused, that rules can be weapons, and that being poor, misunderstood, or angry makes you expendable in this system. I recognized that most of the other inmates could not read or write, and this awakened a sense of mindfulness in me that reminded me of how blessed I am to have my level of intellect and cognizance.

I learned quickly how to adapt. You either hardened, or you were broken. I did what I had to do to survive, but survival is not living, and prison does not teach you how to live. You learn more about how to disappear into compliance.

Gateway Youth Home

By sixteen, I was sent to the Gateway Youth Home. A step down, but still part of the machine. I rose to become the House Coordinator, the highest job function available. I supervised chores. I maintained order. I represented our house when interfacing with the adult facility and peer mentored among other inmates.

Behind the structure and responsibility, I was still a teenager trying to rebuild himself with no blueprint. There was no real nourishment. No healing work. No food that fed the brain. No mentors guiding my purpose. Although the system was broken, I was still succeeding within the confines.

Hidden beneath the concrete and fluorescent lights, Gateway became a strange kind of blessing. For the first time in years, I was able to focus. Free from street noise, toxic patterns, and distractions. I dove into my high school curriculum, completed a full semester without interruption, and earned straight A's. Those grades transferred back home, boosting my cumulative GPA. This was a small but pivotal victory. A spark of academic pride, and whisper that maybe I could still turn this around. My experience represented a fresh possibility.

My Turnaround Story

Eventually, I was placed on house arrest. I could have folded and spiraled the way the system predicted, but something in me refused. I decided I would not let their story about me become my story. That decision changed everything.

Back in school, a turning point arrived when an English teacher saw something in me that others had overlooked. She pulled me from the standard English class and designed a private, college-level study just for me that challenged me. I thrived in this position. She saw not just my potential, but my readiness. She called for a meeting in the guidance office and boldly advocated for my placement in all honors courses. Reluctantly, the administration agreed. From that moment forward, I never scored below one hundred percent in any class. I made high honor roll every semester until I graduated. Had I been challenged, supported, and noticed earlier, I likely would have been valedictorian.

My studies earned me a full-tuition scholarship to a university. I began peer mentoring incoming freshmen who had been placed on the same at-risk list I once appeared on. I volunteered for Big Brothers, Big Sisters. I had found my way out of the system, or so I thought, and spent the next decade walking a new path. I did all of this in spite of the system.

Set Up to Fail Again

Years later, at twenty-eight, I was arrested for cannabis charges. This time, I was not a kid, I was an adult. The system did not see a man trying to do better. They saw a file, a number, and a profit margin. They sent me to prison boot camp, where the goal was not transformation, but domination.

They broke us down with sleep deprivation, humiliation, forced drills with the heat index being too high, yelling, threats, and monotony. I witnessed inmates who gave the guards attitude get beaten to bloody pulp and kicked out of the program to go back to a different prison. We were forced to lay with our nose and toes on the concrete floor while they dumped bleach buckets on the floor to mop. They did everything in their power to break us. There was no therapy. No education. No food that was not poison. This was ritualized suffering.

That experience forged me, because even in the belly of that beast, I saw flashes of truth: *what people could become if someone just gave them a real chance.* I did not mistake escape for arrival. Each small victory in my life, whether an A on a paper, a semester finished, or a younger student mentored, was a stone set into a bridge I was still building as I walked.

The more I chose discipline over drift, service over swagger, and study over survival, the more a new self took shape. One not defined by charges or cages, but by choices. I learned that momentum is medicine: when you move toward what is true, life meets you halfway.

The System is a Funnel, Not a Ladder

What I learned from my journey through incarceration is that the system is built to keep people inside, not help them get out. Once you have a record, doors close. When you get labeled, people stop listening. After they process you, society forgets the person behind the paperwork. That is why I had to build my own ladder. I educated myself. I healed my body. I cleansed from the inside out. I wrote books. I started a business. I became a father, a leader, and a facilitator for healing.

None of this was easy, and most of the people I was locked up with never got the same chance. This is what The Prison Cure represents. We are changing the game from the inside. We are offering transformation instead of torture, nourishment instead of neglect, and empowerment instead of punishment.

From Inmate to Architect

I have seen the inside. I have lived there. Now my plan is to help make improvements. Not with empty reform slogans, better uniforms, or more cameras, but with food, movement, purpose, healing, music, sunlight, and sovereignty.

Every inmate holds the potential to rise, but first, someone must stop burying them under poison and shame. Someone must believe in their ability to rebuild. That is what I am here to do and what this book is for. This is the time to build a new blueprint.

When we walk through fire and survive, we are never the same. The scars we carry are not simply wounds; they are also maps. They remind us of where we have been, but they also point toward where we must go. In this way, suffering becomes a strange kind of compass, quietly directing us back to the truth of our own resilience.

The system may have been designed to break me but also revealed something unbreakable within me. In the silence between punishments, I began to hear another voice. Not the voice of the guards, or of the courts, but the voice of my own soul. He spoke softly, reminding me that dignity is not granted by institutions but is remembered from within.

To live through these cages is to be entrusted with a certain responsibility: *to transform pain into wisdom, and wisdom into service.* My story is not only mine; this belongs also to the countless others still caught inside, waiting for someone to believe in their light. To carry these experiences is to carry a vow that the cycle of suffering will not end with me, but that through me, something new can begin.

Gateway 4: The Mind in a Cage

Why Mental Liberation Must Precede Physical Release

You do not have to be behind bars to be in prison. There is also a prison that wraps around the mind. A cage of thought patterns, learned helplessness, and inherited pain. That prison often stays locked long after the gates have opened and the ankle monitor comes off.

The truth is, incarceration begins in the nervous system. The fight-or-flight that never shuts off. The belief that you are unworthy of better. The voice in your head that says, *"Why try?"* The system knows this and takes advantage of inmates.

How the System Hijacks the Psyche

Prisons are designed to control behavior through fear and routine. Over time, that control seeps deeper, burrowing into thought, posture, and identity. You wake up when they say. You eat what they give. You speak when allowed. You walk in lines. You adapt to survive.

From the outside this may appear as order, but on the inside, there is a slow disintegration of self-trust, self-expression, and autonomy. Over months or years, you start to forget that you are a creative being. You forget that you can build, imagine, love, or lead.

You begin to think in loops:

- *"What is the point?"*

- *"They will never let me out."*

- *"Even if I get out, I will just end up back."*

- *"I do not deserve more than this."*

The longer you are inside, the more you start believing this.

The Cycle of Psychological Entrapment

This is the mental trap that the system thrives on:

Break someone down just enough so that they can function, but not enough that they can flourish. Keep them reactive. Keep them exhausted. Keep them fighting over scraps. Then point to their behavior as proof that they cannot be trusted with freedom.

This is not rehabilitation but domestication through deprivation. Real reform begins with reclamation of the mind.

The Keys to Unlocking Inner Freedom

If we want to liberate those behind bars, we must first teach them how to reclaim their inner authority.

This begins with:

1. Stillness

Time in prison is often loud, chaotic, and overstimulated in all the wrong ways. There is no quiet to meet yourself. No sacred space to breathe. True stillness is the required medicine that allows the nervous system to re-regulate. This invites awareness and creates space between impulse and action.

Introduce breathwork, meditation, and eyes-closed silence. Designate time in nature, even if simply being barefoot under a tree in the yard. These are not luxuries. They are essential nervous system repairs.

2. Movement

When the body is locked down, the mind follows. Stagnation breeds depression. Movement reconnects the brain to breath. Whether with yoga, calisthenics, stretching, martial arts, or dance, movement is sovereignty made visible.

3. Language

Words shape reality. Inmates are often only spoken to in commands, corrections, or criticism. By introducing literature, journaling, poetry, and meaningful dialogue, we begin to return language to a rightful purpose: *transformation*. Give a man words for his pain, and you give him a map out.

4. Imagination

Hope begins in the imagination. When you can no longer envision a life beyond the gate, you stop trying. Art, music, visualizations, and storytelling can reopen the inner cinema. Let inmates dream again of what they could become, of who they already are beneath the scars.

5. Connection

Isolation is the quiet killer of the soul. A man can endure harsh conditions if he feels seen, heard, and valued, but without connection, despair takes root. Connection does not require crowds or constant interaction but authenticity. Circles of trust, mentorship, letters that carry real words, conversations that go beyond surface survival. Connection reminds a person that they are not alone in their struggle and that their story matters.

Prison Can Be a Place of Awakening

Here is the paradox: prison can destroy you or wake you up. I know this because I have lived in both realities. There were moments I almost lost myself and moments when the stillness of that cell gave me the first clarity I had ever known. There were no distractions. No numbing. Just the mirror, my breath, and me, with myself.

No one should have to stumble blindly into awakening. We can design the environment to support transformation. We can make prison a monastery instead of a warehouse. We can provide a dojo instead of a dungeon. This can be a sanctuary for the soul.

The Mind is the First Gate to Open

Physical release means nothing without mental release. You can walk out of prison with the same stories running your life. These are stories of failure, unworthiness, anger, addiction, and despair. Another option is to walk out having rewritten your narrative. Having taken the cage off your mind, even before the door was opened.

The Prison Cure is about the internal revolution that must happen in parallel, not only structural reform. You remember that you are not your record, your trauma, or what they did to you. You are what you choose to reclaim.

True liberation is not the absence of bars but the presence of awareness. A man can sit in a cell and still taste freedom if he knows how to breathe, how to return to the present moment, and how to see his own worth. Likewise, a man can walk freely on the streets and still be imprisoned by anger, fear, or despair. The real walls are not built of concrete, but of stories we believe about ourselves.

The work of transformation begins the moment we notice the gap between who we think we are and who we truly are. To sit in stillness is to glimpse that space. To move the body with intention is to reclaim that space. To speak words of truth is to expand. To imagine new possibilities is to step fully in. These practices are not escape mechanisms; they are the beginning of true return.

If the system insists on cages, then let us teach those inside how to dissolve the cage from within. Let us remind them that their mind is vast, like the sky, and that no wall, no guard, and no sentence can ever contain the sky. When one remembers this, even a single breath can become a key, and even in silence, the song of freedom can begin again.

Gateway 5: Addiction, Survival, and Spiritual Starvation

What We Are Really Punishing and What We Should Be Healing

Behind every prison sentence is a wound, and every addiction, a coping mechanism. There is a story that was never allowed to be heard with compassion that precedes crime. We say we are locking up criminals, yet in truth, we are criminalizing the symptoms of a spiritually starved society.

Incarceration is not just a response to lawbreaking. This has become our culture's default reaction to unprocessed trauma, poverty, emotional pain, addiction, and disconnection from meaning. We punish what we refuse to understand, and we starve the very parts of people that most need to be fed.

The Addicted Nation

Step inside almost any correctional facility, and you will find addiction woven into the fabric. Dependency issues are prevalent, whether through substance use, compulsive behaviors, rage, self-harm, hoarding, control, or emotional withdrawal. Most of these addictions did not start in prison. They started long before.

These are root causes of addiction:

• Children raised in chaos or neglect.

• Teens numbing pain with pills or alcohol.

• Adults coping with hopelessness and broken systems.

By the time someone ends up behind bars, they are often deep in survival mode, their biology and psychology hijacked by stress hormones and neurochemical imbalances. We label them as criminals when we likely should be labeling them as unhealed.

Addiction is Adaptation

Addiction is the symptom, not a disease. This is the result of the body and mind saying, *"I do not feel safe here. I need relief. I need something to fill this hole inside me."* When the only things accessible are sugar, processed food, violence, and distraction, those are what people cling to.

We cannot punish away addiction. This is not a problem that can be caged, humiliated, or shamed out of the body. We must understand and unravel where this behavior is rooted and replace what is depleting with what is nourishing.

The Hunger Is Not Just Physical

Most inmates are spiritually malnourished long before they arrive. They have never had someone truly believe in them or felt seen without judgment. They have not been told that their life holds sacred value. So, they act out, implode, disconnect, or shut down. This is not because they are evil, but because they have never been fed where they require nourishing the most.

We must nurture their:

• Purpose

• Connection

• Stillness

• Beauty

• Hope

• Truth

These are the nutrients of the soul and without them, a person will rot, no matter how clean their urine is, or how well they behave on the tier.

What Are We Actually Punishing?

• When we punish addiction, we are punishing pain.

• When we punish relapses, we are punishing unresolved trauma.

• When we punish defiance, we are punishing unmet needs.

We are taking people who have already been violated by life and violating them again with institutional brutality. We are punishing people not for who they are, but for the coping mechanisms they developed in a system that offered no healing. Then we wonder why recidivism is high, and why people return worse, not better. Why the *"correctional"* model corrects nothing.

What Real Reform Requires

If we truly want to break the cycle, we need to stop asking, *"What crime did you commit?"* and start asking, *"What pain are you carrying? What gift is buried beneath your coping? What do you need to heal?"*

The Prison Cure is intended to awaken responsibility. True responsibility can only rise once a person feels their life has value. Once they are nourished in body, mind, and spirit. Once they have the tools and the environment to transform.

To break the cycle requires:

• Ending food policies that mimic addiction (sugar, caffeine, processed junk).

• Providing trauma-informed education and therapy.

• Replacing punishment with skill-building.

• Rebuilding trust through consistency, not control.

• Offering spiritual practices without dogma: *meditation, breathwork, & sacred silence.*

• Introducing nature, music, movement, and art as daily medicine.

Addiction Loses Power When Purpose is Found

The opposite of addiction is connection, meaning, and having agency over one's own story. Sobriety naturally happens when healthier alternatives are discovered that help a person establish purpose.

Once a person feels like they belong to something sacred, addiction begins to dissolve. This is not because they are being forced to change, but because they have remembered who they are underneath the pain.

This is the kind of reform the country needs. Not more cages but more gardens. Not more surveillance but more service. Not more punishments but more pathways home.

Addiction shows us where love is missing. When someone clings to substances or destructive habits, this does not indicate they are broken, but that they are searching. They are reaching for warmth in a world that has gone cold, and for relief in a world that has denied rest. To heal addiction is to restore love where love has consistently been absent.

True reform begins when we stop asking, *What is wrong with you?* and start asking, *What happened to you?* In that question lies the seed of compassion. When compassion is offered, the nervous system softens, defenses lower, and the heart remembers that numbing is not required to survive.

When people are given the chance to find meaning, generally through art, service, and connection with the sacred, the hunger that once drove their addiction begins to transform. What once was a desperate reaching becomes a steady flowering. This is why healing is not a luxury, but the very foundation of justice. Without this mindfulness, the cycle repeats. When present, the cycle dissolves. I suggest reading my book, *You Are Not Powerless: Twelve Steps to Conscious Recovery*, to learn more about healing addiction through self-mastery.

Part II: The Healing Model

Punishment has proven to be limited. This model breaks bodies but does not restore them. Voices are silenced rather than being helped to find truth. Humans are caged but not taught how to live freely. If we are to move beyond cycles of despair and recidivism, we must dare to imagine something different. Something that heals instead of harms, nourishes instead of depletes, and transforms instead of torments.

The Healing Model begins with the recognition that every person carries a seed of restoration within them. No one is beyond repair. What is missing are the conditions that allow that seed to germinate. Soil, water, light, and care translated into food, structure, purpose, connection, and discipline. When we provide these essentials, even behind walls, transformation becomes inevitable.

This section introduces the Gateways of healing. Pathways that replace despair with dignity, punishment with purpose, and stagnation with growth. They are not luxuries or *"perks"* to be earned but are the baseline of what every human being requires to recover wholeness and to remember their inherent worth.

The new prison paradigm is the path by which prisons can become sanctuaries of reform, and where time served is time transformed. This new approach redirects justice to be measured not by how much suffering is inflicted, but by how much potential is awakened.

To heal does not mean to erase the past, but to meet those experiences with enough light that they no longer dictate the future. This model does not pretend that harm has not been done but refuses to let harm be the final word. Every man and woman who walks into a cell carries wounds, whether personal, ancestral, or cultural. These wounds do not close through punishment. They close when given the tools of nourishment, reflection, and renewal.

Healing is the most resilient level of strength that demands accountability, not as humiliation, but as an invitation to growth. Reforming is to call forth responsibility, not as burden, but as a declaration that one's life still matters. A prison rooted in healing raises the standard, asking everyone to meet themselves fully, to stand upright in their own dignity, and to carry that dignity into community.

The Healing Model reminds us that justice cannot be one-sided. The healing of those behind bars becomes the healing of families, communities, and generations. When the seed of potential is watered inside the walls, the fruit is carried far beyond them. In this way, the work done in confinement ripples outward, transforming not just inmates but the culture that once abandoned them. What begins as an act of restoration in one soul becomes a movement of redemption for the whole.

Gateway 6: The Prison Cure Defined

A Blueprint for Healing the Incarcerated Soul

If punishment worked, we would have less crime. If shame worked, there would be less addiction. If cages healed people, this country would be full of wise men walking out of prison gates transformed. We know this is not the case.

The system is operating exactly as designed: to warehouse the wounded, extract their labor, profit from their despair, and return them to society weakened, unwhole, and often more likely to re-offend. There is nothing broken within their model, the intention simply is not helping to reform. This is why The Prison Cure was born. Not as critique, but as a radical alternative.

What Is the Prison Cure?

The Prison Cure is a reimagined model of incarceration that centers on five pillars:

1. Nourishment of the Body

2. Restoration of the Mind

3. Skill-Building for Purpose

4. Spiritual Awakening and Emotional Healing

5. Environmental and Structural Reform

These are the missing ingredients in nearly every prison and juvenile detention center across the country. They are not luxuries or "rewards." These are biological, psychological, and spiritual needs.

1. Nourishment of the Body

We begin with food, because food is foundation and the greatest indicator of frequency. The frequency we feed determines the behavior we breed. Inmates are fed processed, inflammatory, high-sodium, high-sugar diets that erode gut health, impair brain function, and increase aggression. We are punishing people for behavior that we are biochemically inducing.

The Prison Cure requires:

• Access to whole, plant-based meals.

• Elimination of synthetic preservatives, dyes, and GMOs.

• Fresh produce, ideally grown on site.

• Clean, mineralized drinking water.

• Education about nutrition and detoxification.

• Weekly juice cleanses or fasting options for healing.

2. Restoration of the Mind

The incarcerated brain is often in a constant state of fight-or-flight. Without neuroregulation, rehabilitation is nearly impossible. We do not need more rules. We need mental hygiene and emotional tools.

The Prison Cure integrates:

• Daily breathwork and guided meditation.

• Trauma-informed group therapy.

• Somatic tools for anxiety, anger, and PTSD.

• Reconnection to the body's natural rhythms through circadian awareness.

• Writing and reflection practices to release mental loops.

3. Skill-Building for Purpose

When people have a sense of why, they stop identifying with what they have done. Skill-building is empowerment in action. People leave prison and cannot get hired. This is systemic sabotage, not rehabilitation. We must build humans, not rap sheets.

Prisons should become schools of sovereignty, offering:

• Trade education (plumbing, carpentry, culinary arts, mechanics).

• Language learning and communication skills.

• Financial literacy and business planning.

• Music, art, and creative expression.

• Certifications that lead to employability post-release.

4. Spiritual Awakening and Emotional Healing

Everyone inside is carrying a story. A loss. A betrayal. A wound they were not allowed to speak into the world. The Prison Cure believes healing is impossible without spiritual connection, however this looks for the individual. You are not required to subscribe to a religion to deserve grace or redemption.

This includes:

• Nature exposure (gardens, trees, animals, rivers, and lakes).

• Sacred silence and introspective time.

• Journaling, visioning, and creative visualization.

• Peer mentorship circles.

• Ceremony and ritual to mark progress and growth.

5. Environmental and Structural Reform

You cannot build new lives inside broken buildings. Every square foot of a facility should be designed to remind a person that their life is worth something. Prisons must evolve from punishment chambers to residential healing campuses.

This can be accomplished by implementing these policies:

• Biophilic design (natural light, plants, earth tones).

• Waste reduction (no more Styrofoam, plastic overload, and toxic trash cycles).

• Onsite permaculture and composting.

• Functional movement spaces.

• Safe spaces for personal retreat and solitude.

Accountability Without Abuse

The Prison Cure does not coddle inmates or remove accountability. In fact, this concept demands more of the individual by believing in their power.

Inmates are not just expected to behave. They are expected to build, contribute, grow, heal, and learn. Not through fear, but through structure, support, and expectation born of belief.

The message becomes:

"You are not your past, or your worst day, but you are responsible for who you become next. We will give you the tools to rise."

From Punishment to Possibility

Imagine a system where prisons become incubators of redemption. Where correctional officers become coaches and mentors, not just guards. Where the metrics of success are not recidivism and compliance, but graduation, health, creativity, and peace.

When accountability is paired with opportunity, a man no longer shrinks under the weight of his mistakes but rises under the vision of his potential. A facility rooted in this truth becomes more than a holding pen and can be redirected as a greenhouse for human dignity. Here, every choice is an invitation to reclaim worth, and every skill learned is a brick in the foundation of a new life. This is not leniency; this is leadership, calling forth the highest in a person until they remember that their existence matters, not just to themselves, but to the whole.

This is what The Prison Cure stands for. We advocate for stronger humans, not softer punishments.

Gateway 7: Food as Reform, Not Reward

Why Nutrition is the First Step Toward Transformation

In every meaningful transformation, the body must come first. The body shapes the breath and is the foundation of all change. The breath then shapes the mind, and our mind determines our choices. If we ignore the body, we cannot truly reform anyone.

If we poison the body, three times a day, every single day, we are not reforming a person. We are reinforcing the behaviors, imbalances, and biological dysfunctions that led them here in the first place. This is why food must be at the center of the prison reform conversation. Not as a luxury or a *"perk,"* but as the first tool of healing.

Food Is Chemistry, Not Just Calories

When an inmate eats a tray of processed meat, bleached flour, canola oil, fake cheese, and high-fructose corn syrup, this sets off a chain reaction in the body.

This surfaces as:

- **Blood sugar spikes** → followed by crashes and mood swings.
- **Neuroinflammation** → leading to poor impulse control, fog, and depression.
- **Gut dysbiosis** → breaking down immune health and emotional regulation.
- **Chronic constipation** → from stagnation of toxins and emotional suppression.
- **Fatigue** → stripping the body's ability to handle stress.

These are not side effects. They are biological breakdowns that lead directly to the behaviors the system claims to punish, being addiction, aggression, apathy, outbursts and violence.

A System That Feeds Sickness

Most prisons operate under contracts with food vendors who offer the cheapest per-plate costs, not the most nourishing options.

This results in:

- Ultra-processed slop with almost no fiber.
- MSG-laced soups and fake sauces.
- Moldy bread, expired goods, reconstituted meat.
- Fruit cocktail from a can as the token *"vegetable"*.
- Chemical-laced drink mixes served as hydration.

Why Food Must Be the Reform Foundation

Inmates know they are being poisoned. They taste the deadness and feel the depletion in their bones. Even the commissary, as discussed earlier, is stocked with addictive, low-nutrient products that keep people hooked and inflamed. This is institutional harm, not solely nutritional neglect. The body must be stabilized before the mind can elevate.

If we truly want people to change, they need access to:

• **Whole, living foods:** fruits, vegetables, greens, nuts, seeds, legumes.

• **Raw juices:** rich in enzymes and cellular hydration.

• **Healing herbs:** like dandelion, turmeric, burdock, and ginger.

• **Fermented foods:** for gut-brain balance (kimchi, sauerkraut, miso).

• **Mineral-rich hydration:** clean water with electrolytes and trace minerals.

• **Fasting options:** guided protocols for cellular reset and spiritual clarity.

This does not need to be expensive, just intentional. Imagine inmates growing their own kale, harvesting beets, squeezing citrus, composting leftovers, and learning how to rebuild their body from the inside out. Food becomes more than sustenance. The entire eating process becomes an act of dignity.

Reforming the Meal Model

What if the prison meal schedule looked like this?

Morning: Warm lemon water, herbal tea, soaked chia, and fresh fruit. Cleansing, energizing, digestive awakening.

Midday: Lentil stew, salad bar, steamed vegetables, and quinoa. Sustaining, stabilizing blood sugar, mental clarity.

Evening: Green juice, baked sweet potato, sautéed greens, and herbal broth. Anti-inflammatory, calming, gut healing.

• Add in juice fasts twice a month for those who opt in.

• Add education on how each food heals the body.

• Let food become a conversation, not a punishment.

When food shifts from punishment to empowerment, this rewrites identity. A tray of processed slop tells a person, *"You are worthless."* A tray of color, vitality, and intention tells them, *"You still matter."* Each bite becomes a message that their future is not predetermined, that their body is not disposable, and that their life is still worthy of investment. Food is communication. To reform the menu is to reform the story people believe about themselves.

Food as a Mirror of Belief

When you feed someone garbage, you are saying, *"This is what you deserve."* When you feed someone healing food, you declare, *"I believe in your future."* That message matters.

Most incarcerated people have never been truly fed in their lives. Not just nutritionally, but energetically. They have never been nourished with care or had a plate of food that reflected love, or purpose, or faith in their recovery. The Prison Cure demands we shift from feeding to nourishing.

We already know that food affects behavior. We have data on gut-brain interactions, inflammation and aggression, and serotonin production in the intestines. Prison reform is not lacking science; there is simply a void of soul. There is a lack of the will to do what is right, even if inconvenient.

The real question is not *"Can we afford to feed inmates better?"* The most compelling suggestion is, *"Can we afford not to?"* If we want to reduce violence, suicide, recidivism, and chronic illness behind bars, we must start at the cellular level. Change the food, and you change the person.

Let Every Meal Be a Message

A message that says: *"You are not trash. You are not forgotten. You are not your worst moment. You are alive and you are worth feeding well."* That message, delivered three times a day, is the beginning of true reform.

Every meal is teaching. When a plate carries color, freshness, and care, there is also a whisper to the one receiving, saying: *life is possible, renewal is possible, and you are not abandoned.* When a plate carries only deadness and chemicals, this whispers another message: *you are forgotten, and you are unworthy of vitality.* Reform begins in what we choose to whisper three times a day.

The body is the soil of the spirit. If the soil is depleted, nothing new can grow. If nourished, seeds long dormant will begin to rise. This is not metaphor alone; this is biology, psychology, and spirituality working as one. Food is not just chemistry. Food is relationship. The way we feed others is the way we announce what kind of relationship we want with them.

When we choose to nourish, we are already reforming. To hand someone a living meal is to hand them back a piece of their dignity and to remind them that their story is not finished. A healed plate is a doorway, and when that doorway is opened, the possibility of healing the whole person becomes real.

Gateway 8: Skill Over Sentence

Why Education, Trades, and Creativity Matter More Than Time Served

We fix broken systems by creating opportunities, not counting time. The traditional prison model is built on the assumption that time equals transformation. Serve your time, and supposedly you have paid your debt. We all know better. We know that time alone does not change a person. This can just as easily harden them, numb them, or bury their gifts under routines of survival.

What truly reforms someone is not time but tools. Not just information, but skills, practice, and purpose. A man with a skill has a future. A woman with a trade has sovereignty. A person who knows how to create becomes dangerous in the best possible way: *they no longer need the system to give them their worth.*

Education Is the New Intervention

According to the RAND Corporation, inmates who participate in educational programs are forty-three percent less likely to return to prison than those who do not. Education does not just reduce recidivism but also increases self-worth and restores possibility. Education must go beyond books and worksheets. We must awaken dormant potential. Every hour spent in skill-building is an hour rewriting identity.

The Prison Cure proposes a model where prisons are not stagnant holding tanks, but active academies, offering:

• GED and high school diploma completion.

• Trade school certifications (plumbing, electrical, HVAC, welding).

• Coding bootcamps and digital literacy.

• Nutrition and holistic health courses.

• Foreign language learning (with conversation groups).

• Creative writing, spoken word, and poetry programs.

• Entrepreneurial development and business mentorship.

When education, trade, and creativity become the foundation of reform, prison stops being a warehouse and starts becoming a workshop. Instead of men and women leaving with nothing but a record and a release date, they step out with skills in their hands, confidence in their minds, and purpose in their hearts. This is not leniency but true accountability. When people are given the tools to build, they are also given the responsibility to choose creation over destruction. In this way, every classroom, shop, and studio becomes a seedbed of sovereignty, preparing people not just to reenter society, but to uplift.

Work Without Purpose Is Slavery

Many inmates are forced to work for pennies. They clean, cook, farm, and sew uniforms. While labor can be a noble part of rehabilitation, when compulsory, underpaid, and without educational value, this becomes modern-day slavery.

The Prison Cure flips this model:

• Work is voluntary.

• Work is accompanied by learning objectives.

• Inmates are paid fairly (with scalable wage systems).

• Work leads to certifications, apprenticeships, and career pathways.

• There is transparency around where goods and profits go.

When someone feels like they are being used, resentment grows. When they feel like they are building something of value, their character grows.

Creativity Is Survival for the Soul

Inside every cell block is a hidden artist. A man who writes rhymes on paper scraps. A woman who sketches portraits of people she misses. A teenager who makes beats by tapping his feet on the floor.

Creativity is a form of medicine and is not simply decoration. This is an expression that gives form to feelings too deep for words. This is a way to offer rhythm to chaos, and to help people imagine a future outside of violence and institutional walls.

Creativity breaks the narrative of *"I am just a number,"* and replaces this with *"I am a creator of something real."*

Prisons should be filled with:

• Music programs and drum circles.

• Painting and mixed media.

• Dance, theater, and storytelling.

• Mural projects on cell block walls.

• Open mic nights and publication opportunities.

When work and creativity are reframed as pathways to dignity instead of tools of exploitation, prison culture begins to shift. Men and women who once felt invisible start to recognize themselves as contributors, innovators, and makers. The act of building something tangible, whether a chair, poem, or business plan, plants a seed of self-worth that cannot be taken away by walls or uniforms. In this way, labor and art equip people to reenter society as skilled and confident citizens.

From Certification to Reintegration

True reform does not mean surviving prison, but represents inmates leaving with value in hand, skills under the belt, and a vision forward. This is a system with intention, not a fantasy.

Imagine an inmate walking out of prison not with a parole plan, but with:

• A trade license.

• A resumé.

• Letters of recommendation.

• A job offer from a partnered company.

• A startup business plan and seed funding.

• A language certificate.

• A digital portfolio.

• A published book of poetry.

Skills are Sovereignty

The goal is not just to make people *"behave better."* The goal is to make people capable of choosing better, because they believe they deserve better, and they have been given the tools to demonstrate their value.

• The power of a hammer.

• The dignity of clean code.

• The freedom of speaking multiple languages.

• The pride in earning a paycheck from real work.

• The confidence of building your own small business.

These options provide liberation from despair and debilitating patterns. What if we issue blueprints rather than sentencing time? What if we give inmates not just a second chance but the tools to build a first life they never got?

Reintegration is not about merely opening the gate, but equipping a person to walk through with direction, dignity, and determination. When someone leaves prison carrying certifications, creative works, and skills that translate into opportunity, they are not returning to the same cycle but are stepping into a new identity. This identity is anchored not in their mistakes, but in their capacity to create, contribute, and thrive. A man who has written a book, a woman who has mastered a trade, or a youth who speaks two languages is no longer defined by time served, but by potential embodied. That shift is the true marker of reform.

Gateway 9: Nature in the Cell

Rewilding the Spirit Behind the Walls

Concrete was never meant to hold a soul. Yet, we have built a nation of boxes. Gray, lifeless containers meant to house not just bodies, but potential, memory, and pain. The average prison is a place where nature is kept out and numbness is let in.

What we forget, and what the system forgets, is that healing is a natural process, and nature is the original physician. When you remove sunlight, soil, fresh air, trees, and green, you do not just remove beauty, you also inhibit biology's ability to recover. You remove the cues that remind a human being: *you are still alive.*

The Consequences of Concrete

No matter how strong a person is, they are not meant to exist apart from the earth that birthed them.

Incarcerated individuals live in near-complete separation from the natural world:

• Windows are often small, opaque, or covered.

• Recreation yards are slabs of concrete surrounded by razor wire.

• Green space, if present, is decorative and off-limits.

• Animals are absent.

• Fresh air is recycled and often contaminated.

This sterile, synthetic environment is inflammatory, depressive, and disorienting to the human nervous system.

Nature deprivation leads to:

• Increased aggression.

• Higher cortisol and inflammation levels.

• Disrupted circadian rhythms and poor sleep.

• Vitamin D deficiency and immune dysregulation.

• Depression, anxiety, and despair.

To deprive someone of nature is to sever them from their oldest teacher and most reliable healer. The body may endure concrete, but the spirit longs for soil, sunlight, and sky. When prisons deny this birthright, they do more than strip freedom of movement, they strip freedom of connection. Even the smallest reintroduction of natural elements, a patch of earth to tend or a ray of sun through a window, begins to restore rhythm and hope.

Reintroducing Nature as Therapy

Nature does not have to be wild and expansive to be healing. Even small interventions can begin to restore a sense of calm, curiosity, and life.

The Prison Cure proposes simple, scalable nature integration strategies for correctional facilities:

1. Gardening Programs

• Raised beds, vertical gardens, or greenhouse cultivation.

• Inmates learn to grow herbs, vegetables, and flowers.

• Teaches patience, care, responsibility, and biology.

• Food grown can supplement meals or be donated.

2. Sunlight Exposure

• Scheduled time in open-air spaces with direct sunlight.

• Access to safe outdoor walking or sitting areas.

• Promotion of circadian regulation, vitamin D, and mood balance.

3. Indoor Plants and Biophilic Design

• Strategic placement of living plants in cells, common areas, and libraries.

• Natural materials, colors, and images of ecosystems inside architecture.

• Use of calming earth tones instead of institutional gray.

4. Animal Therapy

• Prison-based dog training programs or therapeutic animal visitation.

• Mutual regulation between inmates and animals fosters trust, empathy, and emotional release.

5. Eco-Restorative Projects

• Inmates participate in restoration of parks, forests, or watersheds post-release.

• Connection to the earth creates a sense of legacy, care, and belonging.

6. Water Access and Flow

• Even the presence of water, whether a small fountain, an indoor aquaponic system, or supervised access to natural bodies of water, can restore calm to the nervous system.

• The sound of running water lowers stress, the sight of reflection soothes the mind, and the act of tending aquatic life teaches harmony and interdependence.

Nature as a Mirror of Self

Nature is a mirror of self. When you work with soil, something changes inside you. When you touch a leaf, breathe in a pine tree's scent, or hear a bird in the distance, you remember something deeper than bars or offenses or names in a file. You remember that you are part of the living world, your breath matters, and your presence still belongs here.

Nature is reintegrative, not just healing. We are reminded that the world does not end at the wall.

Global Examples of Nature-Based Reform

The evidence is clear. When you bring nature in, violence goes down and healing goes up.

Other countries are already doing this:

• Norway's Halden Prison has large windows, forested surroundings, and art on the walls. Their recidivism rate is among the lowest in the world.

• Greenhouse programs in U.S. prisons like Rikers Island and San Quentin have helped inmates find meaning, routine, and emotional grounding.

• Animal fostering programs in places like Washington State have reduced violence and improved social connection inside prisons.

The Cell as a Sanctuary

We are summoning a prison structure that is a place of becoming, not a reform system. This is not rehabilitation if there is no reconnection. We suggest humans be returned to the ecosystem of life, even while behind bars. The most radical thing we can do in a cage is remember the forest.

Imagine a prison where:

• A single plant grows in each cell.

• Sunlight filters in without obstruction.

• The food comes from a garden the inmates tended.

• Murals of forests and rivers line the walls.

• An inmate rises, stretches, touches soil, and waters something living.

• Where he meditates facing a window with a view of trees instead of concrete.

Gateway 10: Discipline as Dignity

Restoring Self-Respect Through Structure and Sovereignty

Discipline is misinterpreted in the modern world, especially in the prison system, where this is often confused with control. There is a vast difference between being controlled by someone else and being in control of yourself. The former is dehumanizing. The latter is dignifying.

That is what The Prison Cure calls for: *not tighter rules, louder commands, or stricter surveillance but a return to internal discipline as an expression of self-respect.* When a person reclaims their own structure, and they begin to keep promises to themselves, they become unbreakable.

Structure Without Soul Is Just Surveillance

Real reform must be chosen. Force never provokes lasting change. The goal in the new paradigm is not to make men docile. The goal is to help them become disciplined enough to direct their lives.

Traditional incarceration relies on external discipline:

• Lights on. Lights off.

• Meals at a bell.

• Count times.

• No talking. No standing. No stretching out of line.

• Obey or be punished.

This kind of rigid control infantilizes and conditions obedience without awareness. A man may become compliant, but inside, he is often still chaotic. He is conforming to a system that was devised from ignorance and offers him no clarity or personal development.

Discipline, when rooted in the soul, is not the iron bar but the bamboo stalk that bends with the storm and rises again with the sun. The quiet agreement between breath and body, a rhythm born from devotion. To wake and make your bed with care is to tell the universe, *I am ready.* To clean your space is to whisper to your spirit, *I honor you.* These small gestures, repeated with sincerity, are not chains of control but threads of freedom, weaving dignity in the fabric of the day.

True discipline is spacious and does not demand submission but invites awareness. This is the art of standing in your own center, steady as a mountain yet soft as flowing water. From here, no guard is needed, and no command required. The man who keeps promises to himself becomes unshakable because his authority comes from within. In this way, discipline transforms from punishment into practice, from surveillance into sovereignty, and from the cage into the key.

The Foundations of Inner Discipline

Discipline is a sacred rhythm, not a military bark. A way of moving through life with awareness and integrity.

The Prison Cure introduces practices of self-discipline that empower instead of diminish:

1. Daily Rituals

This creates a sense of cleanliness, order, and readiness. Not for approval, but for one's own growth.

• Morning silence or prayer.

• Making the bed with care.

• Cold showers (when available).

• Movement or stretching.

• Personal hygiene routines done with pride.

2. Time Ownership

Time stops being a sentence and becomes a resource.

• Using time blocks for study, movement, creativity, and rest.

• Setting personal goals each day.

• Reflection and journaling on progress, setbacks, and focus.

3. Emotional Regulation Practices

This is where reaction becomes response and chaos becomes choice.

• Breathwork for stress and anger.

• Self-inquiry exercises to catch negative thought loops.

• Accountability partnerships within the inmate community.

4. Mindful Speech and Presence

Discipline of language and posture is the discipline of identity.

• Choosing words that build instead of break.

• Speaking truth without violence, and silence without fear.

• Practicing gratitude aloud each day.

• Walking with awareness of breath and body.

• Meeting others with eye contact that communicates respect.

Cleanliness as a Spiritual Act

Cleanliness is not just about sanitation. In environments where decay and dirtiness are common, cleanliness becomes a rebellion of the spirit. This is an inner commitment to care.

Keeping your area clean. Keeping your body cared for. Organizing your books. Cleaning up after others. These are acts of sovereignty in a space that tries to reduce you to survival mode.

Even without control over the building, a person can control:

• How they hold themselves.

• How they treat their own body.

• How they speak, breathe, walk, and rest.

Language and Posture

In prison, falling into speech that is reactive, violent, or resigned is normalized and simplified. To slump, curse, shout, or walk with the body of a defeated man is common and mostly inevitable.

Discipline is choosing your stance in the world, even in captivity. This is not a pursuit of perfection but a representation of persistence in the face of resistance.

The Prison Cure teaches that posture and language create identity.

• Straight spine = clear thoughts.

• Clean words = clear relationships.

• Gratitude spoken daily = a rewiring of perception.

From Control to Command

When a man can govern himself, he is no longer governable by fear. This is why true discipline is liberating. Once you keep your word to yourself, you do not need approval, dominance, or manipulation. You walk with command, not of others, but of your own breath, reactions, and intentions.

This approach to personal discipline cannot be enforced, yet must be invited, modeled, and then cultivated. That is the role of any reform-centered system. To live this way is to become both student and teacher of your own life. Every breath becomes instruction, each step a lesson, and words are mirrors.

Others will notice, not because you are louder, but because you are steadier. This steadiness cannot be taken by force nor broken by confinement but is born in the quiet choice to lead yourself. By doing this, you light a path that shows others what freedom feels like, even before the gates ever open.

Dignity Through Discipline

What we call *"inmate behavior problems"* are often just symptoms of inner disarray. These are men and women who have never been shown how to steward their energy. They require soul cultivation, not just behavioral correction. We can lecture them, punish them, and isolate them, or we can teach them how to rise.

These teachings provide them with the opportunity to:

• Structure their day.

• Master their mind.

• Honor their body.

• Speak with care.

• Clean their space.

• Choose their response.

• Keep their promises.

• Move from impulse to purpose.

Discipline is a compass, not a cage, and will lead anyone, no matter their past, toward a new self. Discipline is the discovery of true freedom. When a person learns to keep promises to themselves, they no longer live at the mercy of moods, impulses, or external control. They begin to walk with steadiness, carrying quiet confidence that cannot be taken away.

Every act of self-discipline is also an act of respect. Making a bed with care, choosing words with clarity, and breathing before reacting are not small gestures. They are reminders that dignity is cultivated one choice at a time. They transform even the simplest routines into ceremonies of sovereignty.

When discipline is rooted in dignity, this ceases to feel heavy and becomes more of a rhythm, like breath or the heartbeat. A current that carries a person forward, even through chaos. In this way, discipline is not punishment, but prayer, and a daily devotion to becoming the person you were always capable of being.

When discipline ripens into dignity, a man no longer measures himself by the bars around him or the judgments spoken over him. He measures himself by the constancy of his own integrity. He learns that freedom is not handed down by courts but grown within, breath by breath, and act by act. This kind of freedom is not dependent on circumstance, so cannot be revoked, and is carried like a flame, steady and silent, illuminating the path forward even in the darkest corridors.

Part III: Rebuilding From Within

The first step of healing is to stabilize the body. The second is to awaken the mind. The final, most essential, and often the most overlooked step is to rebuild from within. This is the stage where true reform takes root, because no external structure, no program, and no policy can carry a man forward if he has not rediscovered his own center.

To rebuild from within is to confront the deeper prison: *the one made of fear, shame, anger, and silence.* This is when you realize that bars and walls may confine the body, but only despair and disconnection truly hold the soul hostage. Freedom, then, cannot be granted by courts or clocks but must be claimed by the individual, moment by moment, until this becomes a way of being.

This is the hardest work, because this requires authenticity. A man can pretend to behave. He can follow rules, recite apologies, and count the days but rebuilding from within demands sincerity and that he stops running from himself. He finally meets the silence he has avoided, the grief he has buried, and the light he has forgotten. This is the path of return.

Within every incarcerated person is a seed of dignity, though often buried under years of trauma, violence, or neglect. That seed cannot be forced open by judgment, but can be coaxed back to life through brotherhood, truth-telling, compassion, and the steady practice of self-respect. When that seed breaks open, something miraculous occurs: *the prisoner does not just reform, he remembers his humanity, his worth, and that he was made for more than cages and labels.*

Rebuilding from within does not excuse past harm but reveals that harm does not have to be the final story. Violence can be transmuted into vitality. Addiction can be redirected into devotion. Silence can be rewritten as song. Rage can be melted into responsibility. These transformations are not theoretical, they are lived, breathing realities when the right conditions are provided. These conditions are not beyond our reach. They are as simple as nourishment, guidance, reflection, and the kind of connection that reminds a man he still belongs to life.

The system as stands is designed to strip away connection and identity but The Prison Cure insists that these elements must be restored. The soul must be taught to taste freedom again, not as license to repeat old patterns, but as sovereignty over the self. Men must be reminded that brotherhood, not bloodshed, is their inheritance. They must be given tools to transform their pain into wisdom, stories into strength, and daily actions into prayers of dignity. This is how the rebuilding begins, not with bricks or budgets, but with the courage to turn inward.

When a man learns to rebuild from within, he becomes more than reformed. He becomes a beacon, a brother, a builder of new worlds. He carries within him the evidence that even in the darkest places, light can return, and that no system, no sentence, and no past mistake is stronger than the soul's capacity to begin again.

Gateway 11: The Soul Knows Freedom

True Liberation Begins on the Inside

One time I was lying in my bunk, staring at the ceiling of a cell I did not choose. The lights were never fully dimmed, the noise never stopped, and the air always carried the residue of sweat, stress, and resignation. Above me, scratched into the underside of the top bunk, someone had carved a countdown: *"14 Days to Freedom."* I remember staring at those words, letting them echo through me. *"Freedom. What did this even mean?"*

I knew something that man did not know yet. You can walk out of prison and still be caged. You can be *"free"* in the eyes of the state but remain enslaved to your addictions, your anger, your trauma, your crowd, your beliefs, and your biology. You can leave confinement and return to the same traps that brought you there, just dressed up in fresh clothes and loud music.

What Is Freedom, Really?

Freedom is not just about walls and gates, or ankle monitors and parole terms. Freedom is clarity. Freedom is choice. Freedom is alignment. Freedom is sovereignty over the self. This does not arrive when a judge signs a paper. This is experienced when the internal patterns that once ruled you begin to dissolve.

Freedom is:

• When the substances lose their pull.

• When the anger cools into self-awareness.

• When the need to impress others is replaced by a quiet knowing.

• When you no longer crave chaos to feel alive.

• When you can sit with yourself and not want to escape.

Real freedom begins when the soul no longer waits for permission. The moment you recognize that your worth is not defined by the charge written on paper or the sentence handed down in court. The instance when you stop bargaining with old habits for comfort and begin to breathe as though each inhale belongs to eternity. This freedom is quiet, and often invisible from the outside, but reshapes everything from within.

When this inner freedom takes root, no circumstance can uproot your liberty. You may still wake to fluorescent lights and clangs of iron, but the weight in your chest is lifted. You may still live under rules you did not choose, but the spirit inside you chooses differently. The body may remain in custody, yet the mind sits beneath an open sky. That is the paradox and the promise: *once the soul knows freedom, no wall can contain you, and no lock can silence your song.*

False Liberation: The Loop of Return

The man who wrote *"14 Days to Freedom"* was already planning his first night out. He spoke of drinks, girls, loud music, and familiar faces. He was carrying the illusion of power. Underneath the facade, I wondered, what would he really return to? A poor diet that weakens his mind? Friends who glorify destruction? Patterns of survival masked as celebration?

What I knew for certain was he would not be leaving with any newly acquired skills. No trade. No tools. No plan. The same unprocessed pain would still be driving his choices.

I thought to myself: *He is not counting down to freedom. He is counting down to another round of the same cage, just without the metal bars.* This is what so many miss: *Freedom is a vibration, not a location.*

If your thoughts are still confined, if your body is still inflamed, and if your identity is still wrapped in pain, you are still in prison. Even if the gates open. Even if the shackles come off.

Internal Liberation Comes First

The Prison Cure begins inside. We know the only freedom that lasts is the kind you create within. Only when the chains that bind you to what lowers your intellect and diminishes your radiance fall, can your steps outside the gate mean something.

We must strive to be:

• Free from processed poison.

• Free from emotional volatility.

• Free from the need to self-destruct.

• Free from the culture that taught you that numbness is strength.

• Free from the cycle of reaction, blame, and violence.

• Free from false narratives about who you are.

This is why so many men leave prison only to find themselves walking back, even without realizing. They are free to move, but not free to choose differently. Their compass is still broken, still magnetized by old wounds and unhealed hunger. True liberation cannot be celebrated in a nightclub or consumed in a bottle. This must be cultivated in the marrow, in the breath, and in the choices that turn a man inward until he discovers a strength deeper than impulse. Without this inner revolution, release is only relocation, and the loop continues.

The Soul Is Not Impressed by Early Release

You can leave prison and still be driven by what put you there. Rather than focusing on *"getting out,"* the emphasis is redirected toward coming back to yourself. A return to the part of you that never had to escape in the first place.

When the soul awakens, the metrics change:

• Silence becomes more valuable than noise.

• Solitude becomes sanctuary, not punishment.

• Health becomes the new high.

• Kindness becomes the act of rebellion.

• Purpose becomes more intoxicating than power.

• Stillness becomes freedom.

Real Freedom Feels Like This:

• Waking up early because you want to.

• Eating food that heals, not numbs.

• Moving with intention.

• Cleaning your space because you respect your surroundings.

• Choosing your words with care.

• Honoring your time.

• Saying no to old triggers.

• Feeling peace even when no one is watching.

This is the freedom no one can revoke. What the system never taught. The paradigm we must begin to model. If a man leaves prison and does not know how to live with himself, he will search for distraction and end up back inside.

The soul knows freedom. If a man finds freedom inside himself, no system on Earth can hold him down. Once he remembers, he cannot be caged again.

Freedom of the soul is not loud, yet this presence transforms everything touched. A man who carries this kind of freedom becomes untouchable, not because he resists the world, but because he no longer needs validation. His dignity is self-sustaining and his clarity self-renewing. This is the kind of freedom that can walk calmly through chaos, breathe steadily in confinement, and still offer light to others in the darkest of places. This is the quiet revolution that turns survival into sovereignty.

Gateway 12: Brotherhood, Not Bloodshed

Connection as the Antidote to Violence

Most of the violence inside prisons reflects pain with nowhere to go. This is not about power. When a person is surrounded by people but never seen, when he is constantly spoken to but never heard, and when his environment expects the worst but never calls out his best, what do you expect him to become?

Too often, prisons breed tension, rivalry, isolation, and suspicion. What people need most is not division. Men require brotherhood. They seek out a sense of belonging. They need someone who sees the man beneath the mask of survival.

I learned firsthand when they put me on a block with a guy who had a reputation. He kept punching people in the face. He was not inclined to talk or smile. He did not want anyone in his space. He was not just angry, he was misunderstood.

The Man Everyone Avoided

Guards thought he was a liability. Other inmates gave him space. They did not see him as dangerous for no reason. They saw a wounded animal in a cage. When animals are wounded and cornered, they strike. Instead of isolating him again, they tried something different.

They thought maybe, just maybe, if he was paired with someone grounded, and someone who carried peace instead of fear, he might change. So, they placed him in the cell next to mine. At first, there were just nods. Cautious proximity. Then came words. Then the gym. Then intellectual conversations.

Concrete and Conversation

Although the *"gym"* was nothing more than a small concrete box with a pull-up bar, that space became sacred ground. We started going there two or three times a day. Not to build muscle, but to build trust. As we sweated in silence, or between reps, he started talking. What he shared once he felt safe and supported did not surprise me. This guy was not just a brawler with a temper. The man was brilliant. He spoke about civil rights, constitutional law, power structures, and injustice with a depth that caught me off guard.

He had lived knowledge, not just book knowledge. He had been burning inside to share this information, but no one had given him the space, or the safety, to speak. All that pent-up wisdom had nowhere to go, so this turned into rage and clenched fists.

With brotherhood, time, space, and respect, this began to transform.

When Words Replace Weapons

The more we talked, the less he fought. The more we built trust, the more his identity shifted. He was not *"that angry brother"* anymore. He was a teacher. A mentor. A man with a mission. He did not need to punch people anymore because someone had finally listened. This is the medicine most men behind bars are starving for. They do not require dominance or threats; they seek acknowledgment.

Once he felt seen, the violence dissolved. Eventually, he was released. From what I last heard, he was living a better life. Still reading. Still speaking. No more fighting. He did not have to fight anymore. He had found a way to belong without bleeding for his prestige.

Brotherhood Heals What Isolation Breaks

True brotherhood behind bars is the strongest force there is. This brings the invisible back into visibility, and centers humanity back into a place that is often forgotten. Brotherhood does not have to come attached to initiation in street gangs either. In addition, those who are affiliated with gangs behind bars can utilize the opportunities within their circles to truly grasp the wisdom and life lessons available within men's work.

What the system fails to grasp is this:

• You cannot punish the pain out of someone but can love the fear out of them.

• You can listen to the rage into softness.

• You can lift someone out of the hole just by sitting with them long enough.

Building Brotherhood as Reform

Not every man is ready for brotherhood right away, but every man is wired to be. Even the most hardened carry the seed that needs to be watered with trust.

The Prison Cure believes every prison should actively create environments where brotherhood and mentorship can flourish:

• Peer-led discussion circles.

• Restorative justice circles and co-listening practices.

• Conflict transformation workshops.

• Inter-generational mentorship pairings.

• Gym partnerships rooted in accountability and emotional safety.

• Spiritual study groups and book clubs.

• Communal service projects where cooperation is required.

We Rise Together

A man does not change because you scream at him. He changes because someone walks beside him in silence long enough for him to remember who he really is. That is what I experienced in that concrete gym. Two men, in confinement, building something freer than any open gate: *A brotherhood. A bridge. A belief in redemption.*

When we stop treating people like problems and start treating them like potential, they rise. Brotherhood is not a strategy, but an innate remembering, which reminds us that beneath every mask of survival there is a human being longing for connection. When two people meet without pretense, or demand, something ancient stirs. The recognition that we belong to one another's company.

Violence fades not when defeated, but when no longer necessary. When a man feels seen, he does not need to shout. When he feels trusted, he does not need to fight. When he feels loved, even in silence, he begins to soften. Brotherhood makes this possible, because brotherhood restores the mirror of dignity.

In this way, brotherhood is both medicine and mirror. This heals wounds of invisibility and reflects the strength a man has forgotten he carries. This camaraderie does not require grand gestures or perfect words. Sometimes, to sit together, to breathe together, or to carry the weight of the day together is enough.

Brotherhood is not built through perfection but through presence. In the willingness to sit with another man in his storms without trying to fix or flee. As a steady hand that does not recoil when rage surfaces but stays long enough for grief to appear beneath. In this way, brotherhood becomes the soil where transformation can take root. Soil that is watered by patience, honesty, and trust.

When that soil is tended, something remarkable happens. Men begin to carry one another's burdens without being asked. They begin to rise not only for themselves but for those beside them. One man's breakthrough becomes permission for another's healing. In this ripple, violence loses grip, and a new story is written. One where men learn that their strength is not measured by how much pain they can inflict, but by how much light they can call forth in another.

When brotherhood takes root, redemption no longer feels like an abstract idea, but this becomes embodied as the way men speak, move, and look at one another. This becomes a new culture, born inside walls that were meant to divide. In this new culture, the possibility of peace is no longer a dream but is a daily practice. To learn more, I suggest reading *Forged: The Twelve Foundations of Manhood.*

Gateway 13: From Violence to Vitality

What Happens When We Choose Health Over Hurt

Violence is not born in a vacuum. This is a symptom, not an instinct. We witness what happens when a nervous system has been trapped in survival for too long. When grief goes unnamed, when pain has no outlet, and when shame curdles into fury.

Most people look at the incarcerated and see a pattern of violence. What they do not see is what came before. The childhood trauma. The malnourishment. The lack of safety. The fatherless homes. The unprocessed loss. The chaos that is being normalized as culture.

If you have never been taught how to live in peace with yourself, how could you ever live in peace with someone else?

The Gateway Stories: Boys in a War Zone

When I was sixteen, I was placed in the Gateway Youth Program. This was a residential facility for troubled youth. I was assigned as the House Coordinator, which meant I had more responsibility, more structure, and in many ways, I was expected to mentor the others. Nothing prepared me for the kind of stories I would hear. I was institutionalized with conditioned criminals, and I was surrounded by wounded kids pretending to be warriors.

There were boys, fourteen, fifteen, and sixteen, telling me about gunfights with their brothers. One kid said he had been shooting at his own sibling, and they both missed, but he had just found out his brother was dead and had been killed by someone else in the streets. He sat there, heavy with guilt, saying, *"That could have been me who killed him. We were shooting at each other like this was normal."*

Another kid talked about watching his cousin bleed out. Another bragged about the size of the gun he had carried before puberty. Another told me he did not expect to live past eighteen. One kid was crying because his second baby was being born, he would miss the birth, and he was only fifteen.

These kids were not monsters. They were boys who never had a chance to heal. Children who had been told that violence was masculinity, that rage was strength, and that numbness was survival. Underneath the tough talk and bravado, though, was pain begging for permission to speak.

What I saw in those boys was not destiny but distortion. Their stories were not prophecies of who they must become, but warnings of what happens when a culture refuses to feed children with love, stability, and truth. Behind every headline of youth violence is a chorus of unheard voices, each one still carrying the possibility of transformation if only given the chance. Violence was never their birthright. This was the language they were forced to learn. Vitality could just as easily be the next language, if only someone taught them how to speak fluently.

From Gunpowder to Green Juice

I believe with every cell in my body that if these boys had been nourished, in mind, body, and soul, most of their violence would have dissolved. Not because they had been scolded, but because they were strengthened from the inside out. You do not have to punch someone to prove you are alive when you are already vibrating with life force. You do not feel a desire to dominate when you feel whole. There is no reason to numb when your cells are clean, your brain is firing, and your heart knows peace.

• What if, instead of fighting each other, these kids were taught how to breathe?

• What if they were fed kale and clean water and real protein instead of ramen noodles and sugar drinks and frozen pizza?

• What if they moved their bodies not to escape trauma, but to process?

• What if they were taught how to stretch, how to fast, how to meditate, how to read, and how to eat for clarity?

• What if we fed them vitality instead of institutionalized despair?

Violence Is Inflammation Turned Outward

We must start seeing violence not as simply *"bad behavior,"* but as a biochemical and emotional imbalance. Those who demonstrate hostility are not evil; they simply have never known true vitality.

These are the conditions that birth rage:

• High cortisol.

• Low serotonin.

• Sleep deprivation.

• Gut inflammation.

• Processed diets.

• Fractured attachment.

• No model of self-regulation.

The truth is that vitality disarms violence before any begins. A child who feels seen, fed, and grounded does not need to raise his fists to be recognized. A teenager whose body is nourished with living food and whose spirit is given outlets for expression does not need to carry a weapon to feel powerful. Strength, when rooted in health and wholeness, expresses in creativity, resilience, and connection. What we label as *"at-risk youth"* are often just undernourished souls waiting to be reminded of their own light.

Vitality as the Antidote

When a person experiences vitality, they are less reactive, less impulsive, and less violent. They become builders, not destroyers. This is why The Prison Cure is not just a food protocol but a peace-building model. We are not simply fighting crime. We are also combating inflammation, spiritual starvation, trauma loops, and cultural conditioning. Vitality is a state of alignment.

We advocate for:

• A clear mind.

• A nourished body.

• A steady breath.

• A sense of purpose.

• A regulated nervous system.

• A relationship with the earth.

• A connection to spirit.

Vitality Replaces the Need to Hurt

When you give people back their vitality, you give them back their clarity. When someone can see clearly, they no longer reach for the trigger. If you want to end the cycle of violence in prisons and neighborhoods, there is no requirement for more batons or stricter rules.

To end the cycle of violence, this requires:

• Greenhouses in every prison yard.

• Breathwork before breakfast.

• Clean food in every cell.

• Healing mentors in every unit.

• Movement that is not punishment.

• Conversations that humanize.

• Rituals that awaken.

• The belief that every man and woman is capable of greatness.

Gateway 14: The Language of Light

Teaching, Guiding, and Purifying from the Inside Out

I never went into incarceration empty. When I stepped into prison, I brought something with me that could not be taken at intake. This was not hidden in my property, or packed in my bag, but carried in my being. I brought light and life-force. Not the superficial kind, but the real. That kind comes from years of purification, from eating clean, and from living with intention. The radiance that burns quietly in the soul of someone who knows who they are, even when the system tries to label them otherwise.

I had entered with clarity, not chaos. With purpose and not panic. People feel this. When I was incarcerated as an adult for cannabis charges, something happened that I now recognize as sacred: *The men around me would gather.*

I realized fast that the other inmates respected knowledge and wisdom. I had brought some of the books I published in with me and gained notoriety quickly for having achieved something that many of them aspired to also accomplish. I had started projects and finished them and earned income in a way that was legal. They flocked to me, not out of fear, but from curiosity. I had earned recognition.

They sensed something different. A man who was not angry. Someone who was not broken. A person who was not pretending to be tough because they were too afraid to feel. They would ask questions, share stories, and sit with me, even if they did not understand why. In places where darkness dominates, the smallest flicker of light becomes a beacon.

A Library in My Bones

I did not just bring my presence; I also brought my books. The books that I had written. Words of wisdom that poured from me during years of clarity and connection to divine truth. Books that held language not of control, but of freedom through purification. I would teach them. Not from a pulpit or with a syllabus but with open hands and real conversations.

I talked about:

• How the body is a temple, and food is the offering.

• How our thoughts carry frequency.

• How breath can break the chains fear cannot.

• How we get closer to God not by fear of sin, but by living in integrity.

• How purification is a form of worship, and cleanliness, both internal and external, is a sacred path back to self.

God Enters Through Purity

The system strips you of so much. Clothes. Autonomy. Space. Comfort. You cannot be stripped of your light, though, if this is real. They also cannot strip you of God, if you know how to listen. What I taught inside was not about religion but was emphasizing resonance.

I shared with other inmates how to:

• Eat in a way that clears the mind.

• Breathe in a way that regulates the spirit.

• Cleanse in a way that opens the heart.

• Forgive in a way that unbinds the soul.

• Speak in a way that uplifts instead of degrades.

When we purify the vessel, we begin to hear the divine frequency again. This frequency speaks in a language deeper than fear and trauma, or bars and uniforms. Divinity speaks in the language of light.

The Respect That Purity Commands

I did not flex my ego, but I carried something that many had not felt in a long time, which was peace. In a place like prison, peace is power. Peace commands presence. Cleanliness becomes an act of quiet rebellion. Stillness becomes magnetic.

I watched as men who had not slowed down in years sat with me to breathe. They started asking what I ate. They began to speak more carefully and pray more frequently. This was not because I told them to. I was leading by example, and they were following my ways. This is likely because when you carry light, you remind others they have radiance too.

Purity enters a room quietly and shifts the atmosphere so even those who have forgotten their own worth begin to sit taller, breathe deeper, and remember. The resonance felt is an unseen current that speaks louder than threats or commands. In the silence of discipline, and in the clarity of clean choices, others see a reflection of what they, too, are capable of.

What commands respect in such spaces is not force but alignment. A man who has stilled his chaos becomes harder to provoke. A man who has cleansed his body becomes harder to break. A man who has remembered his connection to God becomes harder to control. This is the quiet revolution purity ignites: *awakening sovereignty*. Once awakened, this becomes contagious and spreads like light in the dark, reminding every soul touched that freedom begins within.

Teaching as Tending the Flame

We can change a prison with one breath, a single conversation, and the seeds of truth planted in the soil of someone's suffering. I was not there to save anyone, but I was present to reflect on their sacredness. Sometimes this is all they require.

When that seed takes root, and when a man realizes his body is not a burden, but a channel, he harnesses light. When he realizes God is not far, but waiting in his next moment of presence, the life-force within starts to regenerate. When he realizes purity is not perfection, but pursuit, that is when the fire begins to burn. From here, the fire, light, and life-force spreads.

We Are All Teachers in the System

Whether we know this or not, we are always teaching. This is represented in how we carry ourselves, what we say, how we clean our trays, the way we look someone in the eyes, how we eat, how we listen, and how we respond.

The Prison Cure does not just preach reform for the incarcerated. This activates the teachers, healers, and prophets among them. Inside every man is not just a story of survival. There is also a curriculum of light waiting to be lived, spoken, and passed on.

Light is not something we own; this is something we remember. Each time we act with integrity, and every time we choose clarity over confusion, we polish the mirror of our being. In that mirror, others begin to glimpse their own reflection, not as broken or condemned, but as radiant and whole.

The system may attempt to bury light beneath noise, shame, and concrete, but light does not vanish. Your radiance waits. A single spark can guide someone through years of darkness. A single word spoken with sincerity can remind a man that he still belongs to life. In this way, teaching is not about giving knowledge but about awakening what was never lost.

When light is shared, this glimmer multiplies. A man who remembers his own dignity carries this frequency into the yard, into the cafeteria, and into the call with his family. The newfound trust in divinity spreads quietly, and invisibly, until an atmosphere begins to change. This is how transformation truly works. Not by force, but by radiance. When we honor the language of light, even a prison becomes a place where heaven can be remembered.

To teach in this way is not to stand above another, but to walk beside them with presence. Each act of dignity becomes a lesson, every moment of compassion a sermon, and demonstrations of patience a scripture written in real time. In a place designed to strip away worth, the quiet witness of someone living in alignment becomes the most powerful curriculum that tells every watching eye: *you, too, can return to yourself.*

Gateway 15: When the System Cannot See the Soul

The Cost of Dehumanization and the Courage to Rise Anyway

There is a special kind of violence that does not leave a mark on the body but leaves deep bruises on the spirit. This is the violence of being told, repeatedly, *"You are nothing." "You will never be anything." "You are a piece of shit."* I heard this firsthand, every day, in prison boot camp. Not just once, or in passing, but relentlessly. A barrage of psychological warfare designed not to correct, but to crush inmates.

The guards did not speak to us like human beings. They did not call us by name. They spoke in commands, in insults, and in rehearsed humiliation. They told us: *"You do not know anything." "You are worthless." "You will be back." "You are garbage pretending to be a man."*

This was not discipline. This was dehumanization made into policy. I could not help but feel bad for these guards. The inmates were forced to be in this confinement, while the guards chose to come to prison every day. The only difference is they left at the end of their shift to sleep in their own bed at home. They even ate the same food and would order double servings, then boast to other inmates about how they get to have more food. They were just as trapped as us.

When Correction Becomes Cruelty

The boot camp model was built to break, not to teach. They thought that if they stripped us of all pride, all autonomy, and all sense of dignity, maybe we would *"fall in line."* Maybe we would *"learn our lesson."* Shame does not create transformation, though, only disconnection. You cannot call someone trash every day and expect them to become treasure. You cannot treat someone like an animal and expect them to behave like a saint. You cannot heal what you refuse to see.

One guard had a mission to break me. He placed me on "motivation," which was punishment meant for those with bad attitudes, though I did not have one. His real aim was to force me to eat the bologna sandwich that came in the sack lunches for those on motivation, knowing I refused to eat unless they provided vegan food. On the first day of motivation, I threw the sandwich straight into the garbage. He stormed in, cuffed me, and locked me in the transport cage. He told me flatly, *"If you do not eat the meat, you will be kicked out and do five years in prison."* Without hesitation, I refused. Hours later, the superintendent released me, reminding him they could not legally expel me for refusing to eat meat, and quietly commending my courage.

The next day, the same guard placed me on motivation again. He marched me and five others into 106-degree heat, in boots, pants, and long sleeves, conditions so severe that no inmates were supposed to be outside. He gave us sledgehammers and made us hit tires in cadence under the burning sun, waiting for one of us to collapse. Then he came to me, sneering: *"That sledge looks too light for you, Jacoby."* He returned with a welded steel sledge nearly twice as heavy and made me strike large rocks while the others hit the tires. Hours later, he called for a water break. *"Everyone but Jacoby can drink,"* he said. He walked up close, looked me in the eye, and growled: *"You are going to quit or you are going to die, Jacoby."* I looked back without flinching and said, *"Then I will die, Sir."*

I kept swinging until a major arrived and ordered everyone inside because of the heat index. That order might have saved my life. Even in that moment, though, I understood something deeper: *cruelty can try to crush the body but cannot touch the soul of someone who refuses to surrender.*

The System Does Not See the Soul

The system sees the mistake, not the man. The charge, not the childhood. The file, not the future. This is the root of institutional flaws. There is not a person involved in this system who will look in someone's eyes and say, *"There is a soul in there, trying to breathe."* Instead, they declare: *"There is a problem to be controlled."* So, they deny the very thing that makes us human: *Our capacity to grow. To evolve. To shine.*

Mistakes Are Meant to Be Met with Mercy

We have built an incarceration model that treats every mistake like a life sentence. Not in years, but in identity. Mess up once, and you are forever labeled as a criminal, felon, or inmate. Society says, *"You had your chance."* That chance, though, was often given in broken systems, in broken homes, with broken bodies, and unhealed pain.

The Prison Cure says:

• You are not your worst moment.

• You are not what they called you in that cell.

• You are not beyond redemption.

• You are a soul, and souls are built to evolve.

The Need for Expression

In prison, true self-expression is rare. The system does not designate room for this. People want to be heard, known, and seen, but this is not allocated for. When we silence someone's voice, interrupt their story with commands, and label them before they have had a chance to articulate, we lock up more than their body. We also imprison their becoming.

Yet, I have watched what happens when someone is finally given space to speak. To create. To write. To weep. To tell their story without being punished. This is like watching the bars fall from the inside out.

Every Soul Deserves a Chance to Shine

I have seen men written off by society who carried more wisdom than any textbook. I have witnessed broken people becoming builders. I have held space as the hardest exteriors crack open when given a single moment of compassion without agenda. What people need is not to break down further. They require being rebuilt in truth. Once we are seen we start to rise.

Every inmate requires:

• A clean body.

• A quiet mind.

• A safe space to express.

• A sense of divine worth.

• A reminder that they were born with purpose.

• Someone to say: *"I see you. I know you are more than what they say you are."*

Reform Requires Recognition

If we truly want to change the system, we must stop looking at people as liabilities and start seeing them as lighthouses waiting to be lit. Not everyone will change right away, or even at all, but everyone deserves a chance. The real prison is not the cell but the story that says you are unworthy of light. If we can write a new story and create a new system that speaks to the soul, then we begin to resurrect people, not just rehabilitate them.

When we recognize the light in another, we also water the light in ourselves. To see someone as more than their mistake is to bow to the seed of awakening that lives in every being. Even if the seed is buried beneath years of suffering, the potential of this life force is still there, quietly waiting for rain. Reform begins the moment we learn to offer that rain with patience and with trust.

Part IV: The Way Forward

Healing within the walls is not enough if the world outside remains unchanged. A man can learn to breathe again, to eat with clarity, to move with dignity, and to speak with truth, yet if he walks out into a culture that starves his spirit and poisons his body, the cycle will continue. Reform cannot stop at the gate; but must also reach into the neighborhoods, the courtrooms, the schools, the reentry programs, and the policies that shape our collective future.

The way forward is not punishment with a softer name, but transformation that is built into the architecture of justice itself. This requires meals that nourish instead of inflaming, and spaces designed for growth instead of decay. A system that sees every soul, not as statistics, liability, or as a permanent problem, but as a being carrying potential, waiting for the right conditions to rise.

For too long, we have measured success by recidivism rates, compliance charts, and the ability of institutions to maintain order. Order, though, is not the same as justice, and silence is not the same as peace. A prison can be quiet because hope has been extinguished. A parole office can be orderly because fear has taken root. True reform cannot be measured in how still we keep the waters, but in how freely life begins to flow again.

The way forward begins with nourishment of body, of mind, and of community. Food policy is not separate from criminal justice policy. Every tray tells a story about what we believe human life is worth. Every commissary shelf declares whether we are building resilience or dependency. Reform begins when meals become medicine, when gardens replace landfills, and when the biology of healing becomes the foundation of rehabilitation.

The way forward requires new models. Places that do not resemble cages but sanctuaries for transformation. Centers where accountability is not stripped of compassion, where discipline is not divorced from dignity, and where justice does not end with confinement but begins with restoration. We can build alternatives that honor both safety and sovereignty, structures that teach responsibility without erasing humanity. These models already exist in vision, and they can exist in practice if we are willing to invest in transformation instead of perpetuating punishment.

The way forward must also include those who enforce the system. Guards, officers, and staff cannot model humanity if they are living in constant stress, trauma, and disconnection themselves. Healing cannot be selective. When we build systems that nourish the whole, those behind bars and those holding the keys, we end the toxic exchange that corrodes everyone. Reform will fail if dignity is not restored on both sides of the wall.

When the gates finally open, the way forward is measured by what waits outside. Release without preparation is abandonment disguised as freedom. A bus ticket and a plastic bag are not a plan. If we want to end the revolving door, we must replace the current structure with doorways into real life. Housing, mentorship, skills, community, and continued nourishment are required. Exit plans must be more than paperwork; they must be blueprints for possibility.

Ultimately, the way forward is a revolution of redemption. The courage to see people not as the sum of their worst moments but as carriers of potential whose transformation enriches us all. When we redeem the people who society throws away, we are not simply healing individuals, we are healing neighborhoods, families, and futures. Redemption restores the mirror of our shared humanity, reminding us that no life is disposable and no soul is beyond repair.

The way forward requires imagination as much as legislation, and courage as much as funding. We are asked to measure justice not by how well we punish, but by how deeply we restore. To build systems that believe in people more than in cages, in healing more than in harm, and in futures more than in fear.

The way forward is already here, in each act of dignity reclaimed, every meal of real food served, brotherhoods formed, and sparks of light remembered. The question is not whether transformation is possible but whether we have the courage to choose this new path.

The way forward will not be easy and demands that we confront the illusions we have normalized. We are required to admit that punishment has never created peace, that deprivation has never grown dignity, and that cages have never cultivated compassion. There is a need for courage to name these truths in a culture that clings to fear as safety. Yet honesty is the first act of healing, and without this, no system can ever be transformed.

The way forward requires that we think generationally. Every meal denied, each child of an incarcerated parent left unsupported, and all men or women sent back into society broken rather than renewed all ripple into decades of poverty, trauma, and violence. So too does every act of reform ripple forward. A man who learns to cook whole foods behind bars may teach his children how to nourish their bodies. A woman who learns to breathe through her pain may teach her grandchildren how to regulate their emotions. These ripples, multiplied across communities, reshape the landscape of justice.

The way forward requires imagination. A radical willingness to dream beyond cages, barbed wire, and politics of fear. What if prisons became gardens of human potential? What if a sentence became not a punishment but an initiation into a higher version of self? What if the measure of justice was not how effectively we destroy, but how beautifully we restore? To walk this path is to reclaim our role as creators, not just enforcers, and to remember that the systems we live inside of are only as limited, or as expansive, as the stories we dare to write.

Gateway 16: Reform Starts with Nourishment

Fueling Integrity, Healing, and Human Potential, One Tray at a Time

If you want to know the values of a system, look at what they feed people. Most think of food in prison as just bad, but bad does not even begin to describe what is on those trays or delivered as commissary. What the system serves is spiritually corrosive, not just nutritionally bankrupt.

In a place where everything is controlled, including your time, your space, and your words, your food becomes the last thing you can choose to honor your dignity. When even that is denied, this becomes a battle not just for health, but for the soul. I know because I lived through this battle.

Choosing Purity in a System Built on Poison

Throughout my incarcerations, I held fast to one non-negotiable: *I would not eat animal products.* This means no meat, dairy, or eggs. I also refused to ingest processed poisons. There would be no compromises. I did not want to stand out, but my conviction for veganism was, and is, unshakable. Even if this meant starving, being punished, or being broken physically but staying whole in my integrity, there was no way I was budging. I would stay true to what I stand for.

Starving for a Principle

When I was placed in prison boot camp, I faced my greatest test. One of the guards there did not just deny my plant-based request, but he saw this as rebellion. He tried to break me and made extra effort to have me removed from the program. Anyone who did not complete the program would automatically receive a five-year sentence in state prison. He imposed this threat on me simply because I refused to eat meat and dairy.

I did not fight him with words, or beg, or scream, I just stopped eating. For ninety-four days, I starved. I lost forty pounds. and I held the line. I knew I could survive physical hunger, but I could never survive the spiritual sickness of betraying what I knew was right. Not for me. Not for the animals. Not for my lifetime of teachings and writings. Not for the energy I was carrying in that space.

Hunger was my teacher. Each pang of emptiness was a bell of mindfulness, reminding me that the body is not the master of the spirit. With every skipped meal, I touched the truth that real nourishment does not come from food alone, but from fidelity to what is sacred. In that silence, I discovered that to honor one principle deeply is to be fed by an invisible strength greater than flesh.

Finding Grace in the Loudest Place

Before boot camp, I spent time in a state-run prison dorm in Stateville prison, waiting to be transferred. Hundreds of young men were packed into one loud, restless building. The only times we could leave the unit were to hit the gym yard once a day or to serve food trays for the meals. I could not sleep much anyway, because the noise was constant and energy was heavy, so I served. I delivered trays to other inmates for breakfast, lunch, and dinner. Every day, I volunteered.

I was not expecting favors, or reward, but moving with purpose helped me stay sane. I also needed a way to find food I could eat. As servers we could eat extra trays, so I was eating as many of the beans and potatoes as I could get.

The Unexpected Ally

One day, one of the guards saw what I was doing. He knew that I was not causing trouble or complaining. He also found out from other inmates about my books and how I have always eaten healthy and there was a struggle for me to eat well behind those walls. He recognized that I was trying to hold on to my purity in a place built to poison us.

Quietly, without asking for recognition, he started going to the staff salad bar for me. He would bring back a tray filled with raw vegetables. There was lettuce, cucumbers, peppers, broccoli, and tomatoes. That tray represented more than food. This was compassion served cold. Respect without words. For weeks, that is what I lived on before being transferred to the prison camp.

The Food You Eat Becomes the Energy You Carry

The prison system does not just warehouse bodies. People are fed in ways that make them weaker, angrier, more addicted, and less conscious. This is not an accident. There is a model in place that perpetuates this cycle.

They know that when you are inflamed, you do not think clearly. When you are constipated, your emotions stagnate. When you are undernourished, your spirit dims. When your microbiome is overrun by yeast and chemicals, you lose the biological foundation of self-regulation.

I chose differently, even when this hurt, and when I had to go without meals. I knew the real cost of compromising on food was not just weight or strength, but this was compromising my light.

In that season I learned that food was never just about hunger but was also about alignment. Every bite was either a step toward remembering or a step toward forgetting. Even in the loudest, most chaotic places, the quiet act of choosing purity became my protest, my prayer, and my protection. I was reminded daily that while they could control the noise around me, they could not control the frequency within me.

Nourishment Is Reform

Reform must begin on the tray. Not solely by giving inmates better options, but by replacing every meal with an opportunity to rise. This is not luxury, privilege, or reward. This is basic human dignity.

Food is not just what sustains the body, but what sends the soul a message, saying: *"You still matter."*

Imagine this:

- A daily raw food option.

- Detox days with fresh juices and herbal teas.

- Community gardens that provide fresh produce.

- Nutritional education programs led by former inmates turned into healers.

- Fermented foods to heal the gut.

- Clean, structured fasting options for spiritual clarity.

- Water not from lead-tainted taps but filtered and remineralized.

Holding the Line

Even in the belly of the beast, I held the line. I knew something deeper than hunger: *That what I eat becomes what I carry.* I was not going to carry death, fear, or toxicity into my body, even if I had to pay for this with pain.

I believe if others were offered the same opportunity, to choose life, eat in alignment, and rebuild their bodies instead of breaking them, they would change too. Reform does not start with policies. This begins with the plate and what we put inside people. What goes in determines what comes out.

To offer someone food is to offer them a story. One story says, *you are disposable, you deserve only the cheapest scraps.* Another story says, *your life has value, your body is sacred, your future matters.* Every tray carries this choice. Reform begins the moment we choose the second story, repeatedly, until this becomes the culture.

Nourishment is not just about calories or nutrients. This is about the vibration we place into another person's being. A meal can dull the spirit or can awaken. This can inflame anger or cultivate clarity. This can feed despair or remind someone of their inherent dignity. When food is offered with intention, this becomes medicine. When that medicine is given three times a day, every day, this plants the conditions for transformation that no punishment could ever achieve.

Gateway 17: SoulSpire in the Prison System

A Vision Born from Confinement, Built for Liberation

They say necessity is the mother of invention, but sometimes suffering is what gives birth to something sacred. The seed for SoulSpire was planted not in a boardroom, or in a business plan, but in a cell. In a space where men were warehoused like inventory, fed like livestock, spoken to like problems, and forgotten like trash.

The vision for SoulSpire came through, not as a fleeting idea, but as a revelation: *"If no one else is going to create a space that actually heals people, I will."* I saw the void and the obvious need for transformation. After everything I witnessed, including the trauma, neglect, and missed opportunities, I realized that the only way forward was to build something that rewrote the system from the inside out.

SoulSpire Was Forged in the Fire

SoulSpire was born out of my own lived experience through incarceration. This is not based on theoretical perspective. When I entered the system, I was able to understand the business model, recognize the flaws, and devise ways to make improvements. I did not want to just survive the prison circumstances; I also wanted to create something that would make sure the next man did not have to suffer like I did. The inmates require reform in the same way the system does.

I realized prison reform was a necessity from:

• Watching brilliant young men destroy themselves for lack of mentorship.

• Watching trauma erupt into violence because no one taught self-regulation.

• Watching inflammation, rage, and depression spread through processed food and spiritual starvation.

• Watching people leave prison worse than when they arrived.

As I witnessed, I kept thinking: *"This could be different. This could be healed. We just need the right environment."*

The blueprint for SoulSpire was not drawn in ink but in lived memory etched into me by every story I heard, the injustice I endured, and the spark of humanity I saw trying to survive in places built for despair. I imagined how this would look if we turned those sparks into flames, and instead of corralling men into silence, we called them into purpose. If instead of feeding them poison, we nourished them back to clarity. Instead of treating them as liabilities, we invested in them as the leaders, fathers, and healers they were meant to become.

The Original Vision: Alternative Sentencing

The first blueprint for SoulSpire was not a wellness center but an alternative sentencing program. I imagined a place where instead of being sent to a concrete tomb, individuals would be referred by the courts to a living environment designed for healing. This would not be a luxury resort or a fake reform facility, but a real center built on accountability, nourishment, discipline, learning, and soul work. The notion is not simply to keep people out of prison but also assure they never need to go back.

The vision was for SoulSpire to:

• Be funded by the court system, reducing the financial burden on defendants.

• Operate as an inpatient rehabilitation model. A hybrid of wellness retreat, reform school, and sacred initiation.

• Serve as a true sentence replacement for nonviolent offenders and first-time inmates.

• Provide measurable outcomes in recidivism reduction, skill acquisition, emotional stability, and health improvement.

The SoulSpire Model: What is Offered

SoulSpire is more than a brand. This is an ecosystem for human repair. Whether in the current form or as a future expansion into court partnerships, the foundation is the same.

Core Pillars:

1. Plant-Based Nutrition

• Detox protocols, raw food education, juicing, gut repair.

2. Breathwork & Movement

• Daily breath practice, yoga, functional fitness, trauma-informed somatics.

3. Spiritual Development

• Meditation, inner-child work, journaling, sound healing, stillness practice.

4. Trade & Skill Acquisition

• Business mentorship, language learning, holistic health certifications.

5. Community Building

• Brother circles, service projects, conflict resolution, group ceremony.

6. Natural Environment Design

• Biophilic spaces, gardens, clean air, sunlight, living design.

Building the Bridge Between Courts and Consciousness

SoulSpire proves that people do not require more punishment, but they need a path. We want reform that truly reforms.

There is no reason we cannot replace:

• Five years in prison with six months at SoulSpire.

• Juvenile detention with inpatient mentorship and lifestyle redesign.

• Probation check-ins with wellness markers and emotional growth coaching.

They need a place where:

• Their biology is reset.

• Their trauma is heard.

• Their skills are sharpened.

• Their self-worth is restored.

• Their vision for the future becomes tangible.

A Beacon for What's Possible

SoulSpire was never meant to be the exception. This is the prototype. A model that could be scaled and replicated in every state. Adapted to every community and integrated with every forward-thinking court. If we can fund punishment, we can fund transformation. If we can lock people up in cages, we can just as easily open the gates to sanctuaries that set their soul on fire.

The system will not be fixed without a new paradigm, and we are building what the antiquated model refuses to imagine. SoulSpire is proof, not of what we have done, but of what we can become when healing becomes the sentence.

Reform begins with a shift of imagination, not buildings or budgets. The courage to believe that people are more than their worst choices, and that environments can be designed to call forth their highest nature. SoulSpire is more than a program. This is a statement that every life, when nourished and respected, can become medicine for the collective.

The real work of SoulSpire is not simply to keep people out of prison, but to restore their place in the larger fabric of life. When a man learns to breathe again, to eat with clarity, to move with strength, to speak with truth, and to create with purpose, he is no longer a liability. He becomes a living light for his family, his community, and his future. This is how transformation ripples outward: *one restored soul at a time.*

Gateway 18: Healing for Guards and Staff Too

Why the System Breaks Everyone Unless They Choose to Rise

To point fingers at the guards and suggest they are the problem is easy. After everything I have seen, though, and all I have lived through, I have come to understand something deeper: *The system does not just cage inmates.* The enforcers are incarcerated too.

I have watched guards become hardened, violent, sick, and spiritually numb, not because they were born that way, but because the job stripped them of their humanity day after day. The inmates are not the only ones who are starving. The guards are also. They are starving for power, identity, and real nourishment of the body and soul.

When Authority Becomes Abuse

At prison boot camp, I saw things no reform system should ever allow. I saw guards wait for the moment a young inmate would show a flicker of attitude or resistance and then they would strike. They would bark commands, such as: *"About face!" "Turn around!" "No looking!"*

With everyone's backs turned, you would then hear flesh hitting concrete, screams, and a body thudding into the pavement. Then there was silence, followed by the lies: *"He swung first. You saw that, right?" "That inmate attacked me." "He disrespected me."*

We all knew the truth. The guards teamed up, and the inmate never touched them. The punishment for each of these inmates was to be immediate removal from the boot camp program. They were sent back to prison with a longer sentence and had their hope shattered. This was a ritual of domination and not in any way correlated with discipline.

What breaks one side of the bars will eventually break the other. When guards lose their capacity for empathy, they also lose their own humanity. To live daily in an atmosphere of domination and fear is to carry poison in the bloodstream of the soul. Healing cannot be partial. If we wish for transformation, this must include those who wear uniforms as much as those who are identified by number.

Compassion for staff does not erase accountability but does widen the circle of understanding. A guard who learns how to breathe, how to nourish, and how to release his anger without violence, becomes not just healthier himself but a light in a darkened system. When those entrusted with authority rise into wholeness, they stop needing to assert power through abuse. They begin to model the very discipline, dignity, and humanity that inmates are being asked to cultivate. Reform begins to ripple outward from both sides at once.

"Inmates and Animals Only"

The irony was almost too thick to ignore. The same guards who beat inmates were also eating the same expired, toxic food labeled: *"For Inmates and Animals Only."* They would stand in line in the kitchen, proudly loading up trays, saying silly things like: *"Three servings for me today!" "Haha, you only get one!"*

They thought they were winning, but I looked at them, with their swollen bellies, sour skin, twitching nerves, and thinning hair, and I did not feel angry. I felt sadness and a sense of compassion for them. Although they did not see the truth because they slept in a different environment when they left each day, they were also inmates. Incarcerated by their thirst for power and their inability to detach from cruelty and hatred.

Every day, they chose to come back. To wake up and voluntarily re-enter a space of toxicity. To inhale the same dead air, eat the same garbage, and repeat the same scripts. Their sentence was self-imposed. The real tragedy was that most of them thought they had power but what they really had was a badge and a wound.

Juicing and the Ripple of Truth

Not all the guards were beyond reach. Some noticed my movements. The way I centered my breath and prayed before every meal. They saw how I stayed calm under pressure and refused to eat the slop they served. They started asking questions. I shared what I knew about nutrition, plant-based healing, discipline as dignity, fasting, and the gut-brain connection. I talked to them like humans.

Two of those guards started juicing, changed their diets, and quit the prison altogether. They could not stay there once they saw the truth. They could not un-feel what this entanglement was doing to their minds and bodies. That is the power of purity. You become illuminated, not just healed.

Everyone in the System is Wounded

The guard who yells, the officer who hits, and the staff member who lies to keep control are all symptoms of the same disease. They are not the enemy. They are afflicted by disconnection, trauma unaddressed, and a job that chips away at your humanity until violence feels normal and poison feels like a meal.

We must reform the reformers, not only the inmates. They are sick, too, and they deserve better. If we ignore the wounds of those in uniform, we simply recycle pain in a different disguise. A broken officer cannot build whole men, just as a starving healer cannot nourish the sick. True reform must widen the circle to include every soul who walks through those gates, no matter which side of the bars they stand on. Healing must flow like clean water, reaching guards and inmates alike, until the very atmosphere of the prison shifts from a culture of corrosion to a culture of renewal.

A New Role for Correctional Staff

What if guards were trained to be wellness mentors? What if we hired movement facilitators, breathwork guides, clean eating leaders, meditation coaches, and skill-building liaisons? What if their health mattered too? What if their meals were clean, their air fresh, their trauma addressed, and their role repurposed? What if instead of commanding others, they were taught to model leadership from the inside out? This is what The Prison Cure envisions.

We are building a system where:

• Everyone is healing.

• Everyone is growing.

• Everyone is accountable.

• Everyone is a participant in a culture of transformation.

The Wall Can Fall on Both Sides

There is no *"us"* and *"them."* There are only the healed or unhealed. Awake or asleep. Caged or free in the soul. I chose freedom. Even inside the walls. I watched others choose this too, even those wearing the keys.

Let this be the model: *When you change what you put in your body, you change what comes out of your mouth, you change how you treat others, and you change what you return to.* Some will keep coming back to prison, while others will walk out forever, regardless of what side of the bars they stood on.

To heal the system, we must remember that every soul within is a mirror. When one side suffers, the other reflects that suffering. When one side awakens, the other feels the ripple of that awakening. Liberation cannot be selective. We must include those who enforce the rules as much as those who endure them.

A correctional culture that only focuses on compliance creates brokenness on both sides, while a culture that values nourishment, stillness, and dignity can become a sanctuary for all who step inside. Imagine the power of a guard who embodies peace, who models discipline without domination, and who offers presence instead of punishment. Such a presence would not just transform inmates; but would transform the very atmosphere of confinement.

Every act of healing offered to staff is an act of prevention. Every moment of compassion extended to those who carry authority plants seeds of reform for everyone in their care. When we restore humanity to the enforcers, we restore humanity to the system. When humanity is restored, the walls begin to dissolve, even if they still stand in stone.

Gateway 19: Exit Plans, Not Repeat Sentences

Breaking the Cycle of Recidivism with a Real Cure

The doors swing open, and a man walks out. His body is free, but his mind is still chained. He has no job, an unpromising direction, and little support if any at all. He never received a blueprint for how to live. He was provided with a bus ticket, a plastic bag, and maybe a couple dollars on a release card.

He tries to make a life, but his body is inflamed, and his mind is fogged. His community is toxic, and his name carries a record. Eventually he finds his way back into the system. This is the loop. The one we call recidivism. In truth this is a clear reflection of institutionalized failure.

The Truth About Recidivism

Depending on the state, between fifty percent and seventy-five percent of people released from prison return within five years. Some are back within weeks. Others within days. This is not because they want to, but because nothing has changed within them or around them.

You cannot remove someone from a toxic environment, feed them more toxins, deny them purpose, and then expect a miracle. That is not rehabilitation. I would clarify this as recycling pain. The system is not designed to set people free. The design is intended to make people manageable, predictable, and profitable.

Once you are in the system, and you have a number, a file, and a mark, they have a hook in you. You are being reeled back in, not only watched.

A Living Example

Despite being set up for failure, some of us build a new world on the other side after we exit. I know, because I did. To this day, I have been told they use me as an example in the probation office. They say, *"Look what he did. He got through and turned his life around. He got healthy. He built something."*

My story was not experienced because the system helped me, or because I had money or luck. I credit everything to one thing: *Nutrition.*

Food Was My Freedom

Learning how to nourish my body, how to detox, how to cleanse, and how to align my food with my values changed everything. My choice to eat wholesome food at a young age cleared my mind and lifted the fog. This decision gave me strength, clarity, and the biological foundation I needed to evolve.

Once I stopped poisoning myself, I stopped allowing the world to poison me too. That is why I did not go back. I built a foundation they could not take away.

The System Is Set Up for Return

Most people do not get the opportunity that I created for myself. They are released with no plan for nourishment. They receive no mental rewiring, skill set, spiritual grounding, or clarity about who they are. The result is that they fall back into the only world they know. They revert to the relationships they have had. They utilize the only coping mechanisms available.

The system is built to catch them as they fall. Not to catch them to lift them back up, but to bring them back in. A full prison gets funded. A full docket gets staffed. A filled probation pipeline keeps someone's office open. This design operates in a way that provides sustainability for a system that profits from pain.

The Cure Must Be Structural and Spiritual

We cannot simply offer better parole conditions. We need to redefine what a sentence means.

Every inmate needs an exit plan that includes:

• Nutritional detox and education.

• Trade certification or entrepreneurial skills.

• Community reconnection through service.

• Mental and emotional regulation training.

• Continued mentorship and wellness coaching.

• A new environment or housing option away from triggers.

Most of all, they need to believe they are no longer what they were labeled as. That is the essence of The Prison Cure. We are not offering a revolving door. We are advocating for a blueprint, a gateway to a better life, and a living, breathing reclamation of the soul.

Do Not Just Let Them Out, Set Them Free

Freedom is not a bus ride out of prison. This is the opportunity for a rewired nervous system. A regulated gut. A cleaned-up inner dialogue. A skill set. A plan. A tribe. A vision. Until these options are offered, we are not releasing people, we are just pressing pause before the next sentence.

Now is the time to replace recidivism with redemption. This is not to be implemented by hoping for change, but by designing the new model. This will happen, one plate, one breath, and one belief at a time.

Gateway 20: The Revolution of Redemption

Changing the Story, Restoring the Soul, Rewriting the System

At this moment, right now, is our time to dismantle the lies. The lie that says people who have been to jail are broken. The lie that suggests if you have made a mistake, you are forever your mistake. The lie that says incarceration is the mark of a criminal, rather than the symptom of a criminal system.

We have been pointing fingers at people, when the primary problem has been policy, poverty, poison, and propaganda. The system is not *catching bad guys*. They are breeding them.

A Manufactured Criminal Class

We expect people to make good choices, but we give them nothing good to choose from. Then, when they break down, get sick, become angry, lash out, steal, and spiral, we blame them. We lock them up and call them criminals. The real crime is the engineered malnourishment that starts in childhood and never lets go.

We have created a world where:

- The only *"grocery store"* in the neighborhood is a gas station.
- A child's first meal is a bag of chips and a neon-colored drink.
- High-fructose corn syrup is cheaper than fresh fruit.
- Fast food chains outnumber gardens.
- Liquor stores outnumber libraries.
- *"Health care"* means overmedication.
- *"Discipline"* means surveillance, not guidance.

Poisoned, Then Punished

We do not speak enough about what is really driving this epidemic of violence, apathy, and addiction. This is biological warfare disguised as modern life. When people start breaking down, only handcuffs are offered. We do not just punish the poor. We poison them first and then ask why they cannot rise.

The real epidemic is:

- Ultra-processed food that hijacks the brain.
- Synthetic chemicals in every snack, every bottle, every breath.
- Shots and pharmaceuticals are forced into systems already overwhelmed.
- Artificial lights, EMFs, stagnant air, fluoridated water.
- Nervous systems never given rest.
- Gut flora destroyed before the age of five.

The Narrative Must Die

Not every inmate is a bad person. All felons are not dangerous. People who serve time are not always broken. We must change the narrative. Many former inmates are some of the most resilient, brilliant, creative, loyal, and deeply reflective people you will ever meet, they just never had access to real nourishment. Not emotionally, mentally, physically, or spiritually. They have been starved since birth of the sustenance they require.

The Cure Is Nutrient-Based Redemption

If you want to stop crime, start nourishing people, not simply feeding them. They require nutrients, enzymes, minerals, and mentorship, not just calories. Give them sunlight, offer them skill-building, and provide them with clean water and clear thoughts. Give someone a full spectrum of life force and see who they become. When someone is clean in the body, clear in the mind, and centered in the spirit, they do not need to rob, or fight, or escape. They begin to return to themselves, and that return is called redemption.

The Revolution Is Personal

Redemption is not just for the inmate. This enriches society. This adds value for the policymakers, teachers, business owners, families, guards, and for all of us. When one man reclaims his life, he becomes a mirror that reminds the world that we can all change. That no matter how far gone a chance at a good life seems to be, or how dark the path, healing is possible. When that healing is nourished by purity, the revolution within becomes unstoppable.

Building the Cure

Now is our time to destroy the revolving door and end the shame. We have an opportunity to feed the poor before we punish them. We can teach our sons that strength is stillness, and our daughters that dignity is discipline.

This is a call to raise a new generation of men and women who have walked through the fire and come out clearer, cleaner, and freer. We are looking at a model that will turn prisons into sanctuaries and sentencing into transformation. We can convert food into freedom.

We can spark a revolution of redemption. They tried to bury us, but we were the seeds. Now we can germinate in peace and bear fruits of goodness. When the soil is tended, roots are watered, and light and nourishment are offered, growth is inevitable. The same is true for human beings. What the system calls broken is often only buried. What society deems dangerous is often only desperate. What looks like hopelessness is often only hunger, waiting to be met with real sustenance. The cure is found in restoring self-worth and nourishing the body.

Epilogue: The Light They Could Not Take

A Final Note from the Author

I was not supposed to be where I am now, according to the system. I placed my trust in divine orchestration. The system I came through was not designed for people like me to rise. My path and my voice were intended to be silenced, subdued, and cycled through misery. I chose something different. I chose purity.

When I was incarcerated, whether at fourteen, sixteen, or twenty-eight, I refused to let my environment define my evolution. I did not allow the food they served to become my fate. I refused to permit the names they called me to become my identity. I did not let the walls around me block the fire within me.

I healed myself through food. Through breath. Through study. Through stillness. Through devotion to becoming whole again. I watched others sink into the system, not because they were weak, but because they were malnourished in body, in mind, and in soul. I realized the rage, the depression, the confusion, and the hopelessness all start with imbalance. I also saw clearly that this all ends when a person is willing to return to the root.

The Cure is Real

When I began cleansing my body, rebalancing my microbiome, and committing to a plant-based path of integrity, my mind changed. My decisions changed. My destiny changed. This is not theory or wishful thinking. This is what saved me. You cannot think clearly if your gut is full of parasites and pesticides. There is not an easy way to choose peace if your body is inflamed. Access to God can feel challenging even if your vessel is fogged with toxicity. Real prison is enslavement to toxicity. We can break free from this starting today.

The greatest liberation is not walking out of the gate but walking out of illusion. Freedom begins the moment we remember that we are more than what has been done to us, more than the labels placed upon us, and more than the weight of our past. This memory cannot be taken by guards, by courts, or by walls but lives within us like a steady flame.

To heal is to reclaim what was never truly lost. Even in the darkest hours, the seed of light remained intact, waiting for breath, for stillness, and for nourishment. The journey of purification is not about becoming something new but about clearing away what never belonged so what is eternal can shine again. This includes poisons, lies, and fear.

If I leave you with anything, remember this: *you are not broken beyond repair.* The cure is not hidden in distant places or locked in unreachable systems. The remedy is found within your body, your breath, your choices, and your devotion. Begin where you are. Tend to your vessel. Listen to the whisper of the sacred within. The light they tried to take from me is the same light that burns in you.

To Anyone Reading This

Whether you are still behind walls or finally walking free. Whether you are struggling with addiction or just waking up to the idea that you are more than your past. Know this: *Your healing is possible. Your light is real. No matter how far you have fallen, you can rise.*

Your healing begins with food. Practice breathwork. Start with cleaning your space, making your bed, and sitting in silence for five minutes. Start with not letting anyone steal your dignity, not even a system designed to do exactly that. You are the revolution.

Let This Be the Beginning

I wrote The Prison Cure not just to tell my story but to remind you of your story, the one you still get to write. Whether you are a former inmate, a correctional officer, a policymaker, or a son of someone who never came home, you have a role to play in ending the cycle.

This book is a blueprint. The real cure is you. Refuse to let your light be dimmed. Refuse to let poison define your path. Reclaim your purity. Rebuild your biology. Remember, you were born free, now start to live this way.

Healing is a rhythm, not a special event. Some days this feels like progress, while other days like standing still. Acknowledge that even stillness is part of the path. Do not measure yourself by speed but by sincerity. Each choice you make in alignment with truth is a step into freedom that no one can undo.

Remember that no system, no guard, no court, and no mistakes have the final word on your life. The final word belongs to the spark within you. The part that knows you were born for more than cages, labels, and cycles of despair. Protect that spark. Feed your radiance with silence, nourish your essence with clean food, steady your center with breath, and strengthen your ideals with purpose.

You are not only healing for yourself. Each time you choose integrity over impulse, or compassion over cruelty, you help shift the atmosphere around you. You remind others what is possible. In this way, your light becomes contagious. One person returning to the root can change a family. One family can change community. One community can change the culture.

So let this be the beginning, not the end. The Prison Cure is not only a book; this is an invitation. An invitation to step into your own reform, your own liberation, and your own remembering. May you rise with clarity. May you walk with dignity. May your life become the light they can never take.

Closing Meditation & Reflection: Becoming the Light They Cannot Take

This practice is a way to seal the journey of this book into your own body, mind, and spirit. You are invited to move slowly, with presence. Read each step, then pause to practice before moving on. Allow as much time as you need.

1. Find Your Seat

• Sit comfortably with your spine upright but not rigid. Let your feet rest firmly on the ground. Place your hands gently on your lap or over your heart. Close your eyes if that feels safe.

• Take three deep, cleansing breaths. Inhale slowly through the nose, letting your belly expand. Exhale gently through the mouth, releasing tension. Feel yourself arriving in this moment.

2. Breath of Liberation

• Bring awareness to your breath. Imagine that each inhale draws in nourishment in the form of clarity, strength, and peace. Each exhale releases what no longer belongs, being toxins, lies, shame, and fear.

Whisper silently to yourself with each breath:

• Inhale: *I receive what heals me.*

• Exhale: *I release what harms me.*

• Stay with this rhythm for several minutes, until your body begins to soften and your mind feels clear.

3. Remember the Root

• Place a hand on your belly. Imagine a seed of light glowing there. This seed is your dignity and your original wholeness. No guard, no system and no mistake has ever touched this. The seed has always been there, waiting for your care.

• Breathe into that seed. With each inhale, see this grow brighter. With each exhale, feel the warmth spreading through your body, into your chest, into your hands, and into your face.

• Say quietly: *This light is mine. This light is me. This light cannot be taken.*

4. Reflection Questions

When you are ready, open your eyes and take a journal or piece of paper.

Reflect honestly on the following:

• What poisons, whether physical, mental, or spiritual, am I ready to release from my life?

• What practices will I use to nourish myself daily (food, breath, silence, movement)?

• Who in my life could benefit from my light, and how can I share with them?

• What vow am I willing to make to myself today, to walk forward with dignity and devotion?

Write slowly. Let your answers rise like water from a deep well.

5. Closing Intention

• Return to silence for a moment. Place both hands over your heart. Feel your heartbeat as proof that life is still moving through you, that purpose is still calling you.

Whisper:

I am not my past.
I am not my cage.
I am not my pain.
I am light.
I am dignity.
I am free.

• When you are ready, open your eyes.

• Step forward from this practice with calm strength.

• Let your life become the prayer, the medicine, and the proof of the cure.

Final Prayer

May the walls of stone remember silence, and not the cries of despair.

May each bar of iron bend inward, not to trap the spirit, but to remind the heart of an unbreakable light.

To those still confined:

May your breath become your sanctuary. May every inhale be a seed of forgiveness and each exhale a river of release. Though your body is enclosed, may your spirit remain vast as the sky.

To those who govern these halls:

May your newfound wisdom soften your judgments. May justice rise not from punishment but from the soil of understanding. May reform be more than policy alone, but also compassion awakened into action.

To the children who carry the heavy shadows of absence:

May you never mistake your parents' cage for your destiny. May love appear in unexpected guardians, in neighbors, in teachers, and in strangers who choose to see you. May your own hands build a life of wholeness, free from the repetition of chains.

To the world beyond the razor wire:

May we no longer turn away. May we see prisons not as warehouses of the unwanted but as mirrors of what is broken in us all. May healing arrive where vengeance has ruled and may the river of humanity flow again with dignity.

Let the prayer move through every cell, each courthouse, and the restless dreams of children, until the song of freedom is no longer a wish but the ground we walk upon together.

Ten Lessons Prison Taught Me

Prison was initiation for me, not just confinement. I was reminded to step into integrity in a lot of places in my life where I was required to adjust. Most importantly, to be the parent for my children I always needed throughout my childhood and to make a commitment to being present for them in all ways.

While I was stripped of all distractions and left with the bare bones of my being, this I realized was a mirror I could not turn from. Out of the concrete and the silence, these lessons rose, etched not in theory, but in my muscles, my scars, and my breath. They are not only my lessons; they belong to anyone who has suffered, endured, and chosen to rise again.

1. Healing Masquerades as Suffering

When I first entered prison camp, they called us ghosts. For two weeks, we wore all white and stood nose and toes against the wall for twelve hours a day, boots biting into the floor, backs whacked with boards if we slouched. Standing, unmoving, face to wall, with nothing productive to hold onto was one of the hardest things I have ever done. Yet I realized in that pain that my posture, long slouched from years of collapse, was being repaired. Healing often masquerades as suffering. Muscles must ache before they strengthen. Old patterns must crack before new alignment can appear. To endure pain is sometimes the price of remembering how to stand tall.

2. If You Do Not Stand for Something, You Will Fall for Anything

I was tested repeatedly. Guards tried to break my diet, to push me into submission, and to bend my convictions. I refused. Even when this meant hunger or punishment. I learned that when you stand for your principles, whether your food or integrity, you may lose comfort, but you gain sovereignty. Conviction is the compass in a place designed to spin you in circles.

3. Courage Is Expression

Courage is not only in fists or defiance but also in speaking the truth of who you are. In prison, to express a passion, to share a belief, or to reveal softness was often met with ridicule or suspicion. Yet I saw how necessary this was to let courage move through the voice, through art, and through service. Courage is the antidote to invisibility. To live silently in fear is to die daily.

4. Never Give Up on Others

I saw men consumed by rage, addiction, and despair so thick that their light was diffused. Yet, time and again, I watched someone resurrect when offered a little water of kindness. No one is beyond redemption. A single breath of belief, a single gesture of respect, can awaken the seed waiting in the darkest soil.

5. The Body Is a Temple, Even in Captivity

Food was scarce and poisoned, movement restricted, and silence rare, but I discovered the body still listens to how mindful we are of the food we ingest. To refuse poison was to declare, *"I am sacred."* To breathe deeply, even in recycled air, was to remember, *"I am alive."* To cleanse, to stretch, and to move, however small, was to rebuild the altar of the body in a place intent on desecration.

6. Stillness Is Power

Between keys jangling, doors clanging, orders shouted, and televisions buzzing, prison is a combination of lower frequency noises. Yet I found that beneath the chaos, there was stillness waiting to be chosen. To close my eyes, to listen to my breath, and to sit in meditation, even for minutes, was to slip into freedom no guard could touch. Stillness became a form of rebellion, a way to reclaim my mind when everything else was stripped away.

7. Discipline Is Dignity

They tried to use discipline as domination, but I learned that true discipline is self-respect, not punishment. Making my bed with intention, walking with posture, cleaning my space, and moving my body were ceremonies of sovereignty. Discipline is the rhythm that keeps the soul intact when the world tries to unravel.

8. Nature Is the Forgotten Medicine

Even through bars, I searched for green. A blade of grass in the yard, a bird on the wire, the feel of sun across my face. These moments reminded me that I was not just an inmate; I was part of the living world. Nature whispered what the system tried to make me forget: *I belong to life.* Healing requires reconnection to soil, to sky, and to the great rhythm beyond walls.

9. Brotherhood Is Stronger than Bloodshed

Between men clashing and guards asserting dominance, violence was everywhere, but I witnessed how brotherhood could dissolve tension faster than any punishment. When two men sat to talk, to train, and to share ideas, the fists dropped. We are wired for belonging. Brotherhood is the shield that keeps the soul from turning feral.

10. Freedom Begins Within

Perhaps the greatest lesson of all: *you can be caged on the outside and free on the inside, or free on the outside and still caged within.* Real freedom is not beyond the gates or documents but is established in clarity of mind, steadiness of breath, and alignment of choices. The day I realized this; no guard could imprison me again. The walls were still standing, but inside, I was already walking out.

Appendix: Tools for Transformation

Resources, Rituals, and Real-World Practices for Rebuilding from the Inside Out

Appendix A: Daily SoulSpire-Inspired Prison Routine

A sample schedule inmates or program participants can follow to foster discipline, wellness, and self-awareness even within confinement:

Time Practice:

- 6:00 AM Rise, gratitude prayer, silence (5–10 min).
- 6:15 AM Bodyweight movement + breathwork (15 min).
- 6:45 AM Herbal tea or warm water with lemon (if available).
- 7:00 AM Journaling / Morning Reflection.
- 8:00 AM Breakfast (focus on what's clean or minimal).
- 9:00 AM Read something empowering (books, scriptures, poetry).
- 10:00 AM Skill-building or study time.
- 12:00 PM Light stretching, movement, or yard time.
- 1:00 PM Clean space with care and intention.
- 2:00 PM Letter writing / reflection / creativity.
- 4:00 PM Meditation / visualization practice.
- 5:00 PM Nourishing dinner (avoid processed options if possible).
- 6:00 PM Group connection or quiet self-time.
- 8:00 PM Review the day + set intention for tomorrow.
- 9:00 PM Lights out / Deep rest.

Appendix B: Detox & Nourishment Basics

Even in the harshest conditions, the body listens. Small shifts, practiced with patience, become seeds of transformation. Food can be medicine or a poison, and even with limited choices, awareness turns each meal into an act of reclaiming dignity. These principles can dramatically shift biology and mood.

When possible:

• Drink filtered or warm water often (add lemon or apple peels).

• Skip the meat and dairy.

• Choose beans, rice, oats, fresh fruit, or raw veggies over packaged snacks.

• Avoid Kool-Aid packets, fake sugar, or brightly colored drinks.

• Use fasting (if allowed) one day per week as a reset.

• Eat slower. Chew fully. Pray over your food.

• Journal how your body feels after each meal.

Appendix C: Letters from Within (or Space for Reflection)

In the stillness of confinement, words can become wings. A letter written to oneself is more than ink on paper. This is a mirror, a map, and a seed. When the world around you feels unchanging, your voice on the page can be the place where change begins.

Writing is a quiet rebellion against despair that allows you to speak to the future from the present moment, to remind yourself that you are more than your number, your charge, or your circumstance. Each line you write is a step toward freedom, shaping the story of the life you will walk into.

Leave three to four blank lined pages with the heading:

• "What am I choosing to become now?"

• "What truth have I remembered?"

• "What do I want my life to feel like when I leave this place?"

Encourage the reader to write their future into existence.

Appendix D: The Prison Cure Reading List

Books to inspire, awaken, and reform from within:

- *The Raw Cure 2.0* – Jesse J. Jacoby
- *Forged: The Twelve Foundations of Manhood* – Jesse J. Jacoby
- *The Way Knows* – Jesse J. Jacoby
- *You Are Not Powerless* – Jesse J. Jacoby
- *Man's Higher Consciousness* – Hilton Hotema
- *The Four Agreements* – Don Miguel Ruiz
- *The Alchemist* – Paulo Coelho
- *As a Man Thinketh* – James Allen
- *Braiding Sweetgrass* – Robin Wall Kimmerer
- *The Long Walk to Freedom* – Nelson Mandela
- *Letters to a Young Brother* – Hill Harper
- *Autobiography of Malcolm X* – Malcolm X
- *Becoming Supernatural* – Dr. Joe Dispenza
- *The Book of Awakening* – Mark Nepo

Appendix E: Reform Resources & Reentry Support

- Prison Yoga Project – prisonyoga.org.
- Plant-Based for Justice – Nutritional advocacy & support.
- Equal Justice Initiative – eji.org.
- Soul Fire Farm – food justice for people of color.
- SoulSpire (Coming Soon) – Alternative sentencing & healing programs.
- The Last Mile – Tech and entrepreneurship training for inmates.
- Underground Scholars Program – Higher ed reentry for formerly incarcerated.

Appendix F: Court & Legal Models to Watch

Innovative alternative justice models:

• Restorative Justice Circles (vs. punitive sentencing).

• Community Reentry Wellness Hubs.

• Court-Funded Inpatient Programs (like SoulSpire model).

• Post-Release Clean Living Grants (pilot proposal).

Appendix G: Breath & Meditation Basics

Simple practices for regulating the nervous system:

• Box Breathing (4-4-4-4).

• Inhale 4 seconds → Hold 4 → Exhale 4 → Hold 4 → Repeat for 2–5 minutes.

• Stillness Mantra.

"I am not my past. I am becoming my purpose."

Use this during quiet time or before sleep.

Appendix H: Thought Seeds for Daily Reflection

What would my highest self do today?

How can I bring light into this space?

What am I still carrying that I can now release?

What does forgiveness feel like in my body?

What would it mean to walk out of here whole?

About the Author

Jesse Jacoby is a dedicated father and advocate for compassion, equanimity, and purity.

Jesse is the founder and CEO of Soulspire: The Healing Playground (*soulspire.com*). This is a biohacking and purification center with locations near Lake Tahoe in Truckee, CA, and in Nevada City, CA.

Additionally, Jesse is a co-founder of Substance Shield (substanceshield.com), which is an organic, wild-crafted supplement line for replenishing the body before and after substance use.

Jesse is the author of The Raw Cure: Healing Beyond Medicine (1st & 2nd Editions), The Prison Cure: Reform Beyond Incarceration, Forged: The Twelve Foundations of Manhood, The Way Knows: Trusting Divine Orchestration, Where Galaxies Kiss the Earth, The High Life, Windsdom: Wisdom from the Wind, Sovereign Biology, Immune to Fatigue, Modern Human Conditions, You Are Not Powerless, Gaia Speaks, Eating Plant-Based: The New Health Paradigm, & My Quest to Conquer What Matters.

He also co-founded Little Manifestors Publishing and has authored over thirty children's books.

Bibliography

Introduction:

• Alexander, Michelle. *The New Jim Crow: Mass Incarceration in the Age of Colorblindness*. New Press, 2012.

• Davis, Angela Y. *Are Prisons Obsolete?* Seven Stories Press, 2003.

• Eisen, Lauren-Brooke. *Inside Private Prisons: An American Dilemma in the Age of Mass Incarceration*. Columbia University Press, 2017.

• Holt, Jennifer, and Amy E. Singer. "Prison Food as Punishment." *Food and Foodways*, vol. 29, no. 2, 2021, pp. 85–102.

• Pellow, David N. *Total Liberation: The Power and Promise of Animal Rights and the Radical Earth Movement*. University of Minnesota Press, 2014. (Context for environmental burden and landfills).

• Sawyer, Wendy, and Peter Wagner. "Mass Incarceration: The Whole Pie 2024." *Prison Policy Initiative*, 2024, www.prisonpolicy.org/reports/pie2024.html

Chapter One: The Disease of Incarceration

• Alexander, Michelle. *The New Jim Crow: Mass Incarceration in the Age of Colorblindness*. New Press, 2012.

• Bertram, Eva. "Prison Food in America: The Politics of Nutritional Neglect." *Journal of Critical Criminology*, vol. 28, no. 3, 2020, pp. 425–446.

• Holt, Jennifer, and Amy E. Singer. "Prison Food as Punishment." *Food and Foodways*, vol. 29, no. 2, 2021, pp. 85–102.

• Pellow, David N. *Total Liberation: The Power and Promise of Animal Rights and the Radical Earth Movement*. University of Minnesota Press, 2014.

• Sawyer, Wendy, and Peter Wagner. "Mass Incarceration: The Whole Pie 2024." *Prison Policy Initiative*, 2024, www.prisonpolicy.org/reports/pie2024.html

Chapter Two: Processed People, Processed Food

• Alcott, Benjamin, et al. "Nutrition Behind Bars: Addressing the Crisis of Prison Diets." *Public Health Nutrition*, vol. 26, no. 1, 2023, pp. 87–95.

• Eisen, Lauren-Brooke. *Inside Private Prisons: An American Dilemma in the Age of Mass Incarceration*. Columbia University Press, 2017.

• Linden, Meredith. "Food Systems of Control: The Commissary Trap and Inmate Dependency." *Journal of Prisoners on Prisons*, vol. 32, no. 1, 2023, pp. 101–119.

• Nestle, Marion. *Food Politics: How the Food Industry Influences Nutrition and Health*. University of California Press, 2013.

• Richie, Beth E. *Arrested Justice: Black Women, Violence, and America's Prison Nation*. NYU Press, 2012.

Chapter Three: What I Lived Through

• Davis, Angela Y. *Are Prisons Obsolete?* Seven Stories Press, 2003.

• Gilmore, Ruth Wilson. *Golden Gulag: Prisons, Surplus, Crisis, and Opposition in Globalizing California*. University of California Press, 2007.

• Haney, Craig. "The Psychological Impact of Incarceration: Implications for Post-Prison Adjustment." *U.S. Department of Health and Human Services*, 2001.

• Shaylor, Cassandra, and Cynthia Chandler. "It's Like Living in a Black Hole: Women of Color and Solitary Confinement in the Prison Industrial Complex." *New England Journal on Criminal and Civil Confinement*, vol. 24, no. 2, 1998, pp. 385–416.

• Travis, Jeremy, Bruce Western, and Steve Redburn, editors. *The Growth of Incarceration in the United States: Exploring Causes and Consequences*. National Academies Press, 2014.

Chapter Four: *The Mind in a Cage*

• Haney, Craig. "The Psychological Impact of Incarceration: Implications for Post-Prison Adjustment." *U.S. Dept. of Health and Human Services*, 2001.

• Hölzel, Britta K., et al. "Mindfulness Practice Leads to Increases in Regional Brain Gray Matter Density." *Psychiatry Research: Neuroimaging*, vol. 191, no. 1, 2011, pp. 36–43.

• Porges, Stephen W. *The Polyvagal Theory: Neurophysiological Foundations of Emotions, Attachment, Communication, and Self-Regulation*. W. W. Norton, 2011.

• Seligman, Martin E. P. "Learned Helplessness." *Annual Review of Medicine*, vol. 23, 1972, pp. 407–12.

• Shonin, Edo, William Van Gordon, and Mark D. Griffiths. "Mindfulness in Prisons: A Review of the Literature." *International Journal of Offender Therapy and Comparative Criminology*, vol. 57, no. 10, 2013, pp. 1265–80.

• Tang, Yi-Yuan, et al. "Short-Term Meditation Training Improves Attention and Self-Regulation." *Proceedings of the National Academy of Sciences*, vol. 104, no. 43, 2007, pp. 17152–56.

Chapter Five: *Addiction, Survival, and Spiritual Starvation*

• Alexander, Bruce K. *The Globalization of Addiction: A Study in Poverty of the Spirit.* Oxford UP, 2008.

• Felitti, Vincent J., et al. "Relationship of Childhood Abuse and Household Dysfunction to Many of the Leading Causes of Death in Adults: The Adverse Childhood Experiences (ACE) Study." *American Journal of Preventive Medicine*, vol. 14, no. 4, 1998, pp. 245–58.

• Koob, George F., and Nora D. Volkow. "Neurobiology of Addiction: A Neurocircuitry Analysis." *The Lancet Psychiatry*, vol. 3, no. 8, 2016, pp. 760–73.

• Maté, Gabor. *In the Realm of Hungry Ghosts: Close Encounters with Addiction.* North Atlantic Books, 2010.

• Substance Abuse and Mental Health Services Administration (SAMHSA). *Trauma-Informed Care in Behavioral Health Services (TIP 57).* U.S. Dept. of Health and Human Services, 2014.

• van der Kolk, Bessel. *The Body Keeps the Score: Brain, Mind, and Body in the Healing of Trauma.* Viking, 2014.

Chapter Six: *The Prison Cure Defined*

• Andrews, D. A., and James Bonta. *The Psychology of Criminal Conduct.* 5th ed., Routledge, 2010.

• Gesch, Bernard C., et al. "Influence of Supplementary Vitamins, Minerals and Essential Fatty Acids on the Antisocial Behaviour of Young Adult Prisoners: Randomised, Placebo-Controlled Trial." *The British Journal of Psychiatry*, vol. 181, 2002, pp. 22–28.

• Kellert, Stephen R., Judith H. Heerwagen, and Martin L. Mador, editors. *Biophilic Design: The Theory, Science, and Practice of Bringing Buildings to Life.* Wiley, 2008.

• Najavits, Lisa M. *Seeking Safety: A Treatment Manual for PTSD and Substance Abuse.* Guilford Press, 2002.

• Ulrich, Roger S. "View Through a Window May Influence Recovery from Surgery." *Science*, vol. 224, no. 4647, 1984, pp. 420–21.

• Wilson, Edward O. *Biophilia.* Harvard UP, 1984.

Chapter Seven: *Food as Reform, Not Reward*

• Hall, Kevin D., et al. "Ultra-Processed Diets Cause Excess Calorie Intake and Weight Gain: An Inpatient Randomized Controlled Trial of Ad Libitum Food Intake." *Cell Metabolism*, vol. 30, no. 1, 2019, pp. 67–77.e3.

• Jacka, Felice N., et al. "A Randomised Controlled Trial of Dietary Improvement for Adults with Major Depression (The 'SMILES' Trial)." *BMC Medicine*, vol. 15, 2017, Article 23.

• Mayer, Emeran. *The Mind-Gut Connection: How the Hidden Conversation Within Our Bodies Impacts Our Mood, Our Choices, and Our Overall Health*. Harper Wave, 2016.

• Miller, Andrew H., and Charles L. Raison. "The Role of Inflammation in Depression: From Evolutionary Imperative to Modern Treatment Target." *Nature Reviews Immunology*, vol. 16, no. 1, 2016, pp. 22–34.

• Monteiro, Carlos A., et al. "The UN Decade of Nutrition, the NOVA Food Classification and the Trouble with Ultra-Processing." *Public Health Nutrition*, vol. 21, no. 1, 2018, pp. 5–17.

• U.S. Government Accountability Office (GAO). *Bureau of Prisons: Improved Planning and Evaluation Needed to Understand the Impact of Food Service Changes*. GAO, 2016.

Chapter Eight: *Skill Over Sentence*

• California Arts Council and California Department of Corrections and Rehabilitation. *Arts-in-Corrections: California Prison Arts Program Evaluation*. California Arts Council, 2014.

• Davis, Lois M., et al. *How Effective Is Correctional Education, and Where Do We Go from Here? The Results of a Comprehensive Evaluation*. RAND Corporation, 2014.

• Pager, Devah. "The Mark of a Criminal Record." *American Journal of Sociology*, vol. 108, no. 5, 2003, pp. 937–75.

• Western, Bruce, and Becky Pettit. "Incarceration & Social Inequality." *Daedalus*, vol. 139, no. 3, 2010, pp. 8–19.

• Wilson, David B., Catherine A. Gallagher, and Doris L. MacKenzie. "A Meta-Analysis of Corrections-Based Education, Vocation, and Work Programs for Adult Offenders." *Journal of Research in Crime and Delinquency*, vol. 37, no. 4, 2000, pp. 347–68.

Chapter Nine: *Nature in the Cell*

• Berman, Marc G., John Jonides, and Stephen Kaplan. "The Cognitive Benefits of Interacting with Nature." *Psychological Science*, vol. 19, no. 12, 2008, pp. 1207–12.

• Bratman, Gregory N., et al. "Nature and Mental Health: An Ecosystem Service Perspective." *Science Advances*, vol. 5, no. 7, 2019, eaax0903.

• Kaplan, Rachel, and Stephen Kaplan. *The Experience of Nature: A Psychological Perspective.* Cambridge UP, 1989.

• Kellert, Stephen R., Judith H. Heerwagen, and Martin L. Mador, editors. *Biophilic Design: The Theory, Science, and Practice of Bringing Buildings to Life*. Wiley, 2008.

• Odendaal, Johannes S. J., and Roy A. Meintjes. "Neurophysiological Correlates of Affiliative Behaviour Between Humans and Dogs." *The Veterinary Journal*, vol. 165, no. 3, 2003, pp. 296–301.

• Ulrich, Roger S. "View Through a Window May Influence Recovery from Surgery." *Science*, vol. 224, no. 4647, 1984, pp. 420–21.

• Wells, Nancy M. "At Home with Nature: Effects of 'Greenness' on Children's Cognitive Functioning." *Environment and Behavior*, vol. 32, no. 6, 2000, pp. 775–95.

Chapter Ten: *Discipline as Dignity*

• Baumeister, Roy F., and Kathleen D. Vohs. "Self-Regulation, Ego Depletion, and Motivation." *Social and Personality Psychology Compass*, vol. 1, no. 1, 2007, pp. 115–28.

• Deci, Edward L., and Richard M. Ryan. "The 'What' and 'Why' of Goal Pursuits: Human Needs and the Self-Determination of Behavior." *Psychological Inquiry*, vol. 11, no. 4, 2000, pp. 227–68.

• Duckworth, Angela. *Grit: The Power of Passion and Perseverance.* Scribner, 2016.

• Fogg, B. J. *Tiny Habits: The Small Changes That Change Everything*. Houghton Mifflin Harcourt, 2020.

• Tang, Yi-Yuan, et al. "Short-Term Meditation Training Improves Attention and Self-Regulation." *Proceedings of the National Academy of Sciences*, vol. 104, no. 43, 2007, pp. 17152–56.

• Vohs, Kathleen D., and Roy F. Baumeister, editors. *Handbook of Self-Regulation: Research, Theory, and Applications.* 2nd ed., Guilford Press, 2011.

Chapter Eleven: *The Soul Knows Freedom*

• Bowen, Sarah, et al. *Mindfulness-Based Relapse Prevention for Addictive Behaviors: A Clinician's Guide*. Guilford Press, 2011.

• Frankl, Viktor E. *Man's Search for Meaning*. Beacon Press, 2006.

• James, Doris J., and Lauren E. Glaze. *Mental Health Problems of Prison and Jail Inmates*. Bureau of Justice Statistics, 2006.

• Kabat-Zinn, Jon. *Wherever You Go, There You Are: Mindfulness Meditation in Everyday Life*. Hyperion, 1994.

• Ryff, Carol D., and Burton H. Singer. "Flourishing Under Fire: Resilience as a Core of Well-Being." *Psychological Inquiry*, vol. 15, no. 1, 2003, pp. 1–9.

• Ryan, Richard M., and Edward L. Deci. *Self-Determination Theory: Basic Psychological Needs in Motivation, Development, and Wellness*. Guilford Press, 2017.

Chapter Twelve: *Brotherhood, Not Bloodshed*

• Duwe, Grant, and Byron R. Johnson. "The Effects of Prison-Based Faith Programs on Recidivism." *International Journal of Criminology and Sociology*, vol. 5, 2016, pp. 102–18.

• Maruna, Shadd. *Making Good: How Ex-Convicts Reform and Rebuild Their Lives*. American Psychological Association, 2001.

• Pompa, Lori. "One Brick at a Time: The Power and Possibility of Dialogue Across the Prison Wall." *Journal of Correctional Education*, vol. 55, no. 4, 2004, pp. 300–10.

• Sherman, Lawrence W., and Heather Strang. *Restorative Justice: The Evidence*. The Smith Institute, 2007.

• Tutu, Desmond. *No Future Without Forgiveness*. Doubleday, 1999.

• Zehr, Howard. *Changing Lenses: Restorative Justice for Our Times*. 25th anniversary ed., Herald Press, 2015.

Chapter Thirteen: *From Violence to Vitality*

• Felitti, Vincent J., et al. "Relationship of Childhood Abuse and Household Dysfunction to Many of the Leading Causes of Death in Adults: The Adverse Childhood Experiences (ACE) Study." *American Journal of Preventive Medicine*, vol. 14, no. 4, 1998, pp. 245–58.

• McBurnett, K., et al. "Low Salivary Cortisol and Persistent Aggression in Boys Referred for Disruptive Behavior." *Archives of General Psychiatry*, vol. 57, no. 1, 2000, pp. 38–43.

• Miczek, Klaus A., et al. "Neurobiology of Escalated Aggression and Violence." *Journal of Neuroscience*, vol. 27, no. 44, 2007, pp. 11803–06.

• Raine, Adrian. *The Anatomy of Violence: The Biological Roots of Crime*. Pantheon, 2013.

• Satija, Ambika, et al. "Plant-Based Dietary Patterns and Incidence of Cardiovascular Disease." *Journal of the American College of Cardiology*, vol. 70, no. 4, 2017, pp. 411–22.

• Zaalberg, Arne, et al. "Effects of Nutritional Supplementation on Aggression, Rule-Breaking, and Psychopathology among Young Adult Prisoners." *Aggressive Behavior*, vol. 36, no. 2, 2010, pp. 117–26.

Chapter Fourteen: *The Language of Light*

• Andrews, D. A., and James Bonta. *The Psychology of Criminal Conduct*. 5th ed., Routledge, 2010.

• Bandura, Albert. *Social Learning Theory*. Prentice-Hall, 1977.

• Brewer, Judson A., et al. "Meditation Experience Is Associated with Differences in Default Mode Network Activity and Connectivity." *Proceedings of the National Academy of Sciences*, vol. 108, no. 50, 2011, pp. 20254–59.

• Frankl, Viktor E. *Man's Search for Meaning*. Beacon Press, 2006.

• United Nations Office on Drugs and Crime. *The United Nations Standard Minimum Rules for the Treatment of Prisoners (the Nelson Mandela Rules)*. UNODC, 2015.

• Wheatley, Margaret J. *Turning to One Another: Simple Conversations to Restore Hope to the Future*. 2nd ed., Berrett-Koehler, 2009.

Chapter Fifteen: *When the System Cannot See the Soul*

• Goffman, Erving. *Asylums: Essays on the Social Situation of Mental Patients and Other Inmates*. Anchor Books, 1961.

• Haslam, Nick. "Dehumanization: An Integrative Review." *Personality and Social Psychology Review*, vol. 10, no. 3, 2006, pp. 252–64.

• MacKenzie, Doris L. "Boot Camp Prisons for Young Offenders." *Crime and Justice*, vol. 24, 1998, pp. 1–75.

• Sherman, Lawrence W. "Procedural Justice and Police Legitimacy." *Crime and Justice*, vol. 44, no. 1, 2015, pp. 527–79.

• Sykes, Gresham M. *The Society of Captives: A Study of a Maximum Security Prison*. Princeton UP, 1958.

• Zimbardo, Philip G. *The Lucifer Effect: Understanding How Good People Turn Evil*. Random House, 2007.

Chapter Sixteen: *Reform Starts with Nourishment*

• Barnard, Neal D., et al. "A Low-Fat Vegan Diet Improves Glycemic Control and Cardiovascular Risk Factors in a Randomized Clinical Trial in Individuals with Type 2 Diabetes." *Diabetes Care*, vol. 29, no. 8, 2006, pp. 1777–83.

• Cryan, John F., and Timothy G. Dinan. "Mind–Altered Microbes: The Impact of the Gut Microbiota on Brain and Behaviour." *Nature Reviews Neuroscience*, vol. 13, 2012, pp. 701–12.

• Hall, Kevin D., et al. "Ultra-Processed Diets Cause Excess Calorie Intake and Weight Gain: An Inpatient Randomized Controlled Trial of Ad Libitum Food Intake." *Cell Metabolism*, vol. 30, no. 1, 2019, pp. 67–77.e3.

• Monteiro, Carlos A., et al. "Ultra-Processed Foods: What They Are and How to Identify Them." *Public Health Nutrition*, vol. 22, no. 5, 2019, pp. 936–41.

• U.S. Government Accountability Office (GAO). *Bureau of Prisons: Improved Planning and Evaluation Needed to Understand the Impact of Food Service Changes*. GAO, 2016.

• Wilkins, David J., et al. "Plant-Based Diets and Psychological Well-Being: A Systematic Review and Meta-Analysis." *Nutrients*, vol. 11, no. 11, 2019, Article 2711.

Chapter Seventeen: *SoulSpire in the Prison System*

• Andrews, D. A., and James Bonta. *The Psychology of Criminal Conduct*. 5th ed., Routledge, 2010.

• Davis, Lois M., et al. *How Effective Is Correctional Education, and Where Do We Go from Here? The Results of a Comprehensive Evaluation*. RAND Corporation, 2014.

• Kellert, Stephen R., Judith H. Heerwagen, and Martin L. Mador, editors. *Biophilic Design: The Theory, Science, and Practice of Bringing Buildings to Life*. Wiley, 2008.

• National Institute of Justice. "Problem-Solving Courts." *NIJ.gov*, U.S. Department of Justice, 2023.

• Pratt, John, and Anna Eriksson. *Contrasts in Punishment: An Explanation of Anglophone Excess and Nordic Exceptionalism*. Routledge, 2013.

• Shonin, Edo, William Van Gordon, and Mark D. Griffiths. "Mindfulness in Prisons: A Review of the Literature." *International Journal of Offender Therapy and Comparative Criminology*, vol. 57, no. 10, 2013, pp. 1265–80.

• Zehr, Howard. *Changing Lenses: Restorative Justice for Our Times*. 25th anniversary ed., Herald Press, 2015.

Chapter Eighteen: *Healing for Guards and Staff Too*

• Figley, Charles R. *Compassion Fatigue: Coping with Secondary Traumatic Stress Disorder in Those Who Treat the Traumatized*. Brunner/Mazel, 1995.

• Finney, Caitlin, et al. "Organizational Stressors Associated with Job Stress and Burnout in Correctional Officers: A Systematic Review." *BMC Public Health*, vol. 13, 2013, Article 82.

• Litz, Brett T., et al. "Moral Injury and Moral Repair in War Veterans: A Preliminary Model and Intervention Strategy." *Clinical Psychology Review*, vol. 29, no. 8, 2009, pp. 695–706.

• Schaufeli, Wilmar B., and Maria C. W. Peeters. "Job Stress and Burnout among Correctional Officers: A Literature Review." *International Journal of Stress Management*, vol. 7, no. 1, 2000, pp. 19–48.

• Violanti, John M., et al. "Police Stressors and Health: A State-of-the-Art Review." *Policing: An International Journal*, vol. 40, no. 4, 2017, pp. 642–56.

• World Health Organization. *Occupational Health: Stress at the Workplace*. WHO, 2020.

Chapter Nineteen: *Exit Plans, Not Repeat Sentences*

• Alper, Mariel, Matthew R. Durose, and Joshua Markman. *2018 Update on Prisoner Recidivism: A 9-Year Follow-Up Period (2005–2014)*. Bureau of Justice Statistics, 2018.

• Davis, Lois M., et al. *How Effective Is Correctional Education, and Where Do We Go from Here?* RAND Corporation, 2014.

• Pager, Devah. "The Mark of a Criminal Record." *American Journal of Sociology*, vol. 108, no. 5, 2003, pp. 937–75.

• Visher, Christy A., and Jeremy Travis. "Transitions from Prison to Community: Understanding Individual Pathways." *Annual Review of Sociology*, vol. 29, 2003, pp. 89–113.

• Binswanger, Ingrid A., et al. "Release from Prison: A High Risk of Death for Former Inmates." *New England Journal of Medicine*, vol. 356, no. 2, 2007, pp. 157–65.

• Zaalberg, Arne, et al. "Effects of Nutritional Supplementation on Aggression, Rule-Breaking, and Psychopathology among Young Adult Prisoners." *Aggressive Behavior*, vol. 36, no. 2, 2010, pp. 117–26.

Chapter Twenty: *The Revolution of Redemption*

• Gundersen, Craig, and James P. Ziliak. "Food Insecurity and Health Outcomes." *Health Affairs*, vol. 34, no. 11, 2015, pp. 1830–39.

• Landrigan, Philip J., and Richard Fuller, et al. "The Lancet Commission on Pollution and Health." *The Lancet*, vol. 391, no. 10119, 2018, pp. 462–512.

• Monteiro, Carlos A., et al. "Ultra-Processed Foods: What They Are and How to Identify Them." *Public Health Nutrition*, vol. 22, no. 5, 2019, pp. 936–41.

• Marmot, Michael. "Social Determinants of Health Inequalities." *The Lancet*, vol. 365, no. 9464, 2005, pp. 1099–1104.

• U.S. Department of Agriculture. *Food Access Research Atlas Documentation*. USDA Economic Research Service, 2022.

• Walker, Renee E., et al. "Disparities and Access to Healthy Food in the United States: A Review of Food Deserts Literature." *Health & Place*, vol. 16, no. 5, 2010, pp. 876–84.

Epilogue: *The Light They Could Not Take*

• Barnard, Neal D., et al. "A Low-Fat Vegan Diet Improves Glycemic Control and Cardiovascular Risk Factors in a Randomized Clinical Trial in Individuals with Type 2 Diabetes." *Diabetes Care*, vol. 29, no. 8, 2006, pp. 1777–83.

• Black, David S., and George M. Slavich. "Mindfulness Meditation and the Immune System: A Systematic Review of Randomized Controlled Trials." *Annals of the New York Academy of Sciences*, vol. 1373, no. 1, 2016, pp. 13–24.

• Brown, Richard P., and Patricia L. Gerbarg. "Sudarshan Kriya Yogic Breathing in the Treatment of Stress, Anxiety, and Depression." *Journal of Alternative and Complementary Medicine*, vol. 11, no. 4, 2005, pp. 711–17.

• Cryan, John F., and Timothy G. Dinan. "Mind–Altered Microbes: The Impact of the Gut Microbiota on Brain and Behaviour." *Nature Reviews Neuroscience*, vol. 13, 2012, pp. 701–12.

• Hall, Kevin D., et al. "Ultra-Processed Diets Cause Excess Calorie Intake and Weight Gain: An Inpatient Randomized Controlled Trial of Ad Libitum Food Intake." *Cell Metabolism*, vol. 30, no. 1, 2019, pp. 67–77.e3.

• Longo, Valter D., and Mark P. Mattson. "Fasting: Molecular Mechanisms and Clinical Applications." *Cell Metabolism*, vol. 19, no. 2, 2014, pp. 181–92.

• Mostafalou, Sara, and Mohammad Abdollahi. "Pesticides and Human Chronic Diseases: Evidences, Mechanisms, and Perspectives." *Toxicology and Applied Pharmacology*, vol. 268, no. 2, 2013, pp. 157–77.

• Miller, Andrew H., and Charles L. Raison. "The Role of Inflammation in Depression: From Evolutionary Imperative to Modern Treatment Target." *Nature Reviews Immunology*, vol. 16, no. 1, 2016, pp. 22–34.

www.ingramcontent.com/pod-product-compliance
Lightning Source LLC
Chambersburg PA
CBHW081649270326
41933CB00018B/3405